AVIAT IN BIRMINGHAM

Geoffrey Negus & Tommy Staddon

**AVIATION
IN
BIRMINGHAM**

Foreword

by

Bob Taylor MBE

Director
Birmingham International Airport

Writing this in my office in the new terminal building, which is to be formally commissioned by Her Majesty the Queen on 30 May 1984 — air transport operations commenced here only last week — it gives me enormous pleasure to welcome a book providing such a comprehensive history of aviation in the immediate area of this Airport.

People tend to say that aviation is only 80 years old, but what they really mean is that powered flight by heavier-than-air machines has been going on for only that long, flying itself is much older - we are about to celebrate 200 years of flight in the Birmingham area alone!

My own interest and enthusiasm for the subject started both here and at Castle Bromwich, although I have to say that my first flight was 'round the Tower' at Blackpool in a Rapide some years later.

Although this Airport is now one of the few major centres for flying in the Midlands, this was not always the case. The numerous airfields and aircraft factories which produced thousands of aircraft and employed tens of thousands of people have gone, or are now put to other uses. The happy times - and occasional tragedies, are remembered by many, and this book will, no doubt, revive some fond boyhood or wartime memories.

The authors have gathered an enormous amount of information and have put a great deal of time and effort into producing a book that I am sure will make fascinating reading, especially for those who have had even the most fleeting relationships with airfields or aircraft in this region.

Bob Taylor.

*Title page photograph:
Birmingham International
Airport's new terminal, in
operation on 9 April 1984.
(Geoffrey Negus)*

*First published 1984 by
Midland Counties Publications,
24 The Hollow, Earl Shilton,
Leicester, LE9 7NA, England.*

*Printed in the United Kingdom
by David Green Printers Ltd,
Newman Street, Kettering,
Northants.*

*Bound in the United Kingdom
by F F Allsopp & Company Ltd
Union Road, Nottingham,
Notts, NG13 1FU.*

ISBN 0 904597 51 2

Introduction

This study traces the development of aviation in the Birmingham area from the balloon ascents of the 1780s to the opening of the magnificent new terminal at Birmingham International Airport almost two centuries later.

The story of Birmingham's aeronautical heritage has not been a favourite topic for historians - far more, for example has been written about Manchester. Perhaps this is because no great innovator worked in Birmingham in the early days - a curious fact, considering the city's engineering traditions, and one lamented as long ago as 1910. Another factor might be that although Birmingham made an enormous material contribution to British air power in both World Wars, many of the thousands of Brummies who made aircraft, engines and components were employed by firms not immediately associated with aviation - notably Austin.

Neglected the subject might be, dull it is not. The incredibly daring exploits of the first balloonatics - the excitement of the Edwardians at seeing Claude Grahame-White arrive all the way from London - the massive aircraft construction programmes during the wars - the long struggle to put Birmingham on the world airline map: all have been fascinating themes to research.

We have tried to serve two distinct readerships - the serious aviation enthusiast looking for detail and the local resident interested in Birmingham's past, perhaps remembering his or her own share in it. We hope we have not been too ambitious and failed to satisfy either.

The geographical limitations are not consistent and should be justified. Early flying at Dunstall Park is described because the Midland Aero Club, which was responsible for it, was based in Birmingham. Purists should note that Castle Bromwich aerodrome was not in Birmingham until it was about twenty years old, and even today much of Birmingham International Airport is outside the city boundary! It is hoped that a future volume will deal with aviation in the entire West Midlands area.

We apologise for any mistakes. The authors would be delighted if readers would please come forward with any relevant material they might have.

April 1984

Geoffrey Negus
Tommy Staddon

Acknowledgements

We are grateful to the many people who supplied information and photographs for this book.

Bob Taylor MBE, Director of Birmingham Airport, was always a valued source of encouragement and advice. The Airport Committee Chairman, Councillor Colin Bearwood, was instrumental in securing West Midlands County Council support for our project. His colleague Councillor Vic Turton also took a keen and active interest.

Out thanks go to: Colin Aldridge, John Bagley BSc (Science Museum, London), J S Beach, Roy Bonser, Len Brice, Joan M Brown, M Butler, S S Caro, Barry Chare, Miss Patricia Cooper, Anders Clausanger (British Motor Industry Heritage Trust), Cdr Cedric Coxon MVO, RN (Ret'd), Capt T J Dixon (GKN), Mrs Peggy Donaghy, Henri Ducommun (Midland Aero Club), David Gent (formerly of Lucas), Delwyn Griffiths, Willoughby Gullachsen, Capt Trefor Jones (Birmingham Executive Airways), Lt Cdr L J Kelly DSC, RN (Ret'd), B S Kirkland (Royal Air Force Association), A Luker (Qantas), Capt D G Lusher (British Airways), John Marks, Alec Matthews, John McMillan (Lucas), E B Morgan, Capt Jack Muldoon (Central Air Services), Peter G Murton BA, ALA (RAF Museum, Hendon), Mike Newell, John Nicholds, David Partington (Air-Britain), Colin E Read, Steve Richards, Ian Scott-Hill (British Airways Museum), Charles Simpson, A E Sinton (lately Chairman, Levis Holdings), Frank Sutherland, Bruce Tanner (Horizon), J P Terry (KLM), Ron Thairs, Albert Turfrey, Ron Wilson (Historical Aviation Service) and Derek P Woodhall.

Also thanks to the Birmingham Post & Mail Ltd (especially Mrs Hazel Kennedy), the Local Studies Department of Birmingham Central Library (Mr Patrick Baird) and the Birmingham Museum of Science and Technology (Mrs Brooks and Mr P Robinson). Mention should also be made of the enthusiasts group, Midland Counties Aviation Society, whose monthly magazine *Air-Strip* has for many years recorded local aviation history as it is made.

Gratitude rather than convention dictates that we thank our wives, Yvonne and May, for their encouragement during the writing of this book.

The Authors

Geoffrey Negus, 33, is a television journalist with a life-long love of aviation. He has contributed aeronautical items to most of the programmes he has worked on, which include 'Nationwide', 'Tonight', 'Format V', 'Magic Micro Mission' (which he edited) and 'Venture'. Most of his free time is devoted to researching and writing about aviation - several of his articles have appeared in *Air Pictorial*. In 1980 Geoffrey Negus won the Argos Consumer Writers' Awards for exposing mass counterfeiting by the Taiwanese and other Far Eastern nations.

Born in Cardiff some 70-odd years ago, Tommy Staddon has spent well over 30 years in civil aviation. Throughout the Second World War he served with BOAC in Africa and the Middle East, and joined British European Airways on its formation in 1946. In 1949 he came to Birmingham to launch the first post-war scheduled service from Elmdon, to Paris. He stayed in the Midlands for many years, first as Station Superintendent at Birmingham Airport, then as District Sales Manager for the Midlands, Wales and South West England. When he retired in 1974 he was British Airways manager in Luxembourg.

Origins

The Birmingham Lunar Society, the remarkable scientific society that involved such great thinkers and innovators as Matthew Boulton, James Keir the chemist, Joseph Priestley, James Watt and Josiah Wedgwood, was greatly interested in balloons and flight. Their interest stemmed from their studies of gases - some of which, like hydrogen, were known to be lighter than air. Priestley experimented with 'dephlogisticated air' (oxygen) in 1774. The fashionable response in England to the news of the successful balloon ascents in France in the summer of 1783 by the Montgolfiers was to scoff. But the members of the Lunar Society were fascinated. Within months they were experimenting - though, it should be stressed, there is no record of any of them actually making ascents themselves.

Boulton used balloons to amuse his children, but also attempted serious experiments. On 26 December 1784 his friend James Watt, who lived at Handsworth Heath, wrote to Dr James Lind of Windsor describing an 'inflammable-air' balloon made the previous summer: 'The history of Mr Boulton's explosive balloon is as follows:- He made a balloon of thin paper, and varnished it with an oil varnish. The size was about 5 feet diameter. It was filled with a mixture of about one part common air, and two parts inflammable air from iron. In the neck of the balloon he tied a common squib, or serpent, to which was fastened a match of about two feet long, which made very quick at the end next the serpent. When the balloon was filled, the match was lighted, and the balloon was launched. The night was very dark, and nearly calm; but the match being cut rather too long, it was about five minutes before the explosion took place, in which time the balloon had got about two miles from the place it was let off. A considerable number of people were assembled to see the experiment, and as they lost sight of the match soon after the balloon was let go, they expected it was gone out, and that they should see or hear no more of it; but when the match kindled the serpent, their murmurs were turned into joy, which they expressed by a general shout; which happening when the balloon exploded, the noise of the explosion was very indistinctly heard; though the people, who happened to be in the neighbourhood of it when it exploded, said that it made a noise like thunders, and almost as loud. Indeed they took the balloon for a meteor, and

the explosion for real thunder. Our intention in the experiment was, to determine whether the growling of thunder is owing to echoes, or to successive explosions; but by means of that illtimed shout the question could not be solved, otherwise than by the report of those who were near it, who said that it growled like thunders; but their observations upon it were very inaccurate, and rendered more so by their being unprepared for such a phenomenon. I was not at the place the balloon was let off from, but was at my own house, which is at least three miles from the place where the explosion happened. All I could observe was, that the expolsion was very vivid and instaneous; it seemed to last about one second, and the materials of the balloon taking fire, exhibited a fine fire-work for a few seconds more. These are all the particulars which I remember, or are of any consequence to be known, in a matter so easily repeated'.

The first English aeronaut was James Sadler, who on 4 October 1784 ascended at Oxford. In November *Aris's Gazette,* the Birmingham newspaper, reported, 'The balloon with which Mr Sadler, of Oxford, lately ascended, will next week, with the whole of the apparatus, be brought to this Town and exhibited in the Theatre, and two gentlemen will, in a short time afterwards, ascend with it from this place'.

This news was followed by the advertisement, dated 25 November: 'Mr Sadler, of Oxford, presents his compliments to the Ladies and Gentlemen of Birmingham, and its neighbourhood, and respectfully informs them that the Grand Balloon, with which he attended the twelfth of this instant, at Oxford, is now suspended at the New Theatre, and will be exhibited for public inspection, together with the car and the whole of the apparatus, every day, from ten in the morning till eight in the evening (when himself and his brother, will personally attend), previous to its ascending from a convenient place in the vicinity of this town. Persons desirous of gratifying their curiosity by examining this splendid machine, are requested to attend as early as possible, or they will have no opportunity of seeing it here after it has ascended. - Admittance One Shilling each'.

The brave aeronaut to go up in Sadler's balloon was a Mr Harper. The balloon was moved from the Theatre to the Tennis Court in Coleshill Street, and the following advertisement appeared: 'December 20, 1784 - Mr HARPER repectfully informs the Public, that the exhibition of his Balloon closed on Saturday last for a few days; that he will unavoidably be at a very great Expense in fitting up the Tennis Court, and filling the Globe; he therefore wishes those Ladies and Gentlemen who wish to encourage him, and intend honouring him with their company on the day of his Ascending, the 29th instant, will apply as early as possible for Tickets'.

On 3 January 1785 the Gazette reported that 'strangers of every denomination' came to Birmingham to see Harper's attempt, but 'unfortunately through a failure in the process, it was found impossible to launch the machine that morning. As soon as this was known to the surrounding multitude, they assailed the scaffolding erected for the accommodation of those who had paid for seeing the balloon filled, at first throwing sticks and stones over it, and at length proceeding to pull it down'.

A riot broke out; four of the trouble-makers, one of whom suffered a fractured skull, were arrested. The balloon was rushed away from the Tennis Court before the mob got in. The second attempt was fixed for the following Tuesday, 4 January, 'which we doubt not but will succeed, from the united endeavours of several scientific gentlemen who have undertaken to assist Mr Harper'. The bells of St Philip's Church were to be rung an hour before the attempt.

James Keir, Dr Withering and Mr Southern of the Lunar Society, and 'other scientific gentlemen had kindly undertaken to superintend the filling of the machine, which was completed by 12 o'clock. It was foggy and raining, but one of the biggest crowds ever seen in Birmingham had turned out. Harper, having been presented with flags by lady admirers, took off soon after 1215. It rose for a few seconds, then suddenly descended towards spectators on ground behind the Tennis Court. Harper threw out some ballast, then ascended rapidly in a North by North-West direction. After 1½ minutes he was gone from view. For the first six minutes of the flight, rain fell heavily. Four minutes later Harper shot above the cloud into sunshine. He climbed gradually for about 30 minutes, during which time he estimated he rose 4,300 feet. At Trentham in Staffordshire he flew low to shout through a 'speaking trumpet' for his location. At about 2 pm he descended at Milstone Green, near Newcastle-under-Lyen (sic), after 88 minutes'. During the trip he took bottles of air collected at different altitudes for Dr Priestley, but about a mile from where he finally came to a stop the balloon basket struck a tree and they were smashed. The basket was almost totally destroyed by hedges and trees and it took the local blacksmith to pull it to a stop. That evening Harper and his balloon went to Lichfield and he arrived back in Birmingham the next morning, where he was drawn by the populace (who took his horses from the carriage)

in triumph through the streets.

Harper's flight inspired various poems, many by ladies. 'Emma' wrote,

Hail! favour'd youth, Britannia's future boast,
The Muse's favourite theme,-The Fair-One's toast,
Whose towering spirit, fearless, mov'd along
Heaven's wide expanse-to please a gazing throng;
While to retard thy flight, and aid thy fears,
Aurora frown'd-then softened into tears.

A second ascent was to have been made on Monday 31 January but was delayed until the next day, because the high wind made it impossible to fill the balloon. On the Tuesday, the Gazette reported, 'Mr Harper was seated in the car, the gentlemen who attended deeming the machine sufficiently inflated; but they found it impossible, from the pressure and intrusion of the company (which had all along impeded operations) to ascertain with any degree of certainty, the power of the balloon's ascent, and the quantity of ballast with which it should be charged. Under this and other disadvantageous circumstances it was launched, and driven with some violence against the high wall of the Tennis Court, which, however, it cleared, and was descending, when Mr Harper throwing out some ballast, it was carried with rapidity in an horizontal direction, by a brisk wind, against a garret window in an adjacent yard. In this situation it continued some time, and a large rent having been made in the machine, which was much agitated by the wind, the company at the window seized Mr Harper's arm, and forcibly took him out of the car. An attempt was now made to bring the balloon to the Tennis-Court, to repair the damage it had received, and a man entered the car to keep the machine down, to which also a cord was affixed for that purpose; but by some accident the cord was broken, and the balloon, ascending with the man in the car, was carried over the street and several back houses into a garden, where the populace pursued it, and taking all the ballast out of it, they finally let off the machine, which bearing away in a S.S.E. direction, flew with great velocity, and was in a few minutes out of sight. No accounts have yet been received where it fell'.

A later newspaper report revealed, 'The Balloon dropped at Chippenham, about 14 miles from Bath, where it was found by country people, who suspended it in a barn, and exhibited to strangers at one penny admittance'.

Inevitably, fire balloons became the great amusement of the boys of the time, endangering hay stacks and farm produce. A guinea reward was offered for information on offenders.

In May 1785 a balloon that had ascended from Bristol and travelled twenty-nine miles in half an hour and was now owned by a native of

Birmingham, Mr Cracknell, was exhibited in the theatre in King Street. It was claimed to be the smallest that had carried a man, measuring only twenty-one feet across and having a circumference of sixty-three feet. It was made of 'Gold Beater's Skin' and ornamented with stars. Cracknell asked a shilling from ladies and gentlemen and sixpence from children and servants to view the balloon, but a later announcement indicated that the interest was disappointing.

Dr Erasmus Darwin of the Lunar Society speculated on the practical applications of flight - he corresponded with Edgeworth, another intellectual of the day, about the possible agricultural use of balloons as fertilizer carriers and spreaders. Edgeworth wrote several papers for learned societies recommending a direction guidance system for balloons and in 1817 actually subscribed £50 to the formation of an Aeronautical Society.

Sadler, the first English balloonatic, made flights in Norfolk, the Thames Estuary area, Manchester and Worcester in the 1780s. His second flight from Worcester took him to Lichfield (and thus presumably close to Birmingham), where he tried to land. He was badly injured when he was dragged for five miles until he fell out. The balloon shot upwards, never to be seen again. Sadler retired from ballooning for several years.

Musical festivals were staged to raise funds to enable hospitals to treat those who could not afford medical care, and balloon ascents often featured at them. On 23 September 1811 the *Birmingham Gazette* reported, 'to afford the numerous assemblage of company (attending the Festival) the utmost satisfaction... Mr Sadler will add the sublime spectacle of an ascent of his balloon, which surpasses in size and construction all that have gone before it'. It was described as being thirty-four feet in diameter, forty feet high and made of 4,000 sq ft of silk. It took 25,000 cu ft of gas to fill it and weighed 1,500 lb. The car was lined with yellow silk and elegant cushions, with a covering of azure blue and stars. The rail was of Chinese fretwork and at each corner were the Prince Regent's plumes. 'The whole presents one of the most superb objects which the ingenuity of man can devise, or which the fancy of the spectator can hope to see realised'. On 7 October Sadler ascended with a Mr Burcham and was swept 112 miles in eighty minutes by a gale - almost certainly the fastest journey yet survived by man. In trying to land in Lincolnshire Sadler was thrown out and Burcham carried on for another one and a half miles until an ash tree caught the balloon and tore it to pieces.

In 1823 the Birmingham Gas Company donated £11 to the festival, being the amount received for filling Mr Sadler's balloon. (Sadler died in 1828). In 1829 George Green donated '½ net profits attending his ascent on Saturday October 10', which amounted to £16 11s 2d (£16.56).

Eighty years pass before the next known link between the city and aviation. In April 1909 the Society of Motor Manufacturers and Traders (which today organises the Motor Show at the NEC) staged the first British Aero Show, at Olympia. One of the dozen or so British 'aeromotors' on display was a water-cooled Wolseley 50 hp example, built by the Vickers subsidiary, the Wolseley Tool & Motor Co at Adderley Park. It had eight cylinders, weighed 300 lb, cost £600 and was guaranteed for four hours. This V-type engine had already been bought by the Aeroplane Construction Co for a 'flyer' they were building for trials.

Another exhibit from Birmingham at Olympia in 1909 was a model built by Alfred P Maxfield of 171 Highfield Road, Saltley, who won a Bronze Medal from the Aero League Club. Maxfield was to be Birmingham's first fixed-wing aviator. He built 9 hp engines and put them in two aircraft in his small workshop in Aston Road. The first was wheeled in semi-secrecy to the Castle Bromwich playing fields, but it never flew, and neither did his second. But, as will be related, he was eventually successful.

Blériot's Channel flight a few months later sparked a surge in public interest in aviation. It was in part stimulated by the unpleasant realisation that while Britain might rule the sea, it certainly did not rule the air. Government spending on aviation was stepped up and newspapers sponsored races and new projects.

Wolseley announced in August that it would make the engines for a huge new rigid airship ordered by the Admiralty, and that it planned to tender for the engines required for a National Airship sponsored by the *Morning Post* newspaper. (In the event it was powered by Panhards). By this time Wolseley had supplied engines for aircraft owned by Prof Huntingdon, an aeronautical innovator from Yale University, and Mr Pitman, plus another for an aircraft being built in France. *Flight* on 7 August 1909 described how Wolseley engines were tested: 'Each engine is rigged up upon a specially constructed motor car chassis, and is there fitted with a fan brake, adjusted to a known horse-power. The chassis is then driven at high speed round and round an uneven track during the whole time the engine is under test, and thus is not only working under approximately the same conditions that it would be on a flyer, but is being subjected to a continuous series of shocks of considerably greater magnitude than in ordinary use'. By December 1909 Wolseley were advertising a 180hp engine for dirigibles. It had eight cylinders, cast in pairs, and weighed 600kg. The following month they boasted that a 60hp engine had powered de Baeder's aircraft at Mourmelon when he won four prizes in a single day. Three types of Wolseley engine were displayed at the second Olympia show, in March 1910: a 30hp with four cylinders giving 42bhp at 1,100 revs, the eight-cylinder 50-60hp one and a slightly larger 60hp model.

Other Birmingham firms were by then attacking the blossoming aviation market. The Central Novelty Co of 93 Cornwall Buildings, Newhall Street, offered 'any quantities of Aero Fabric, Wood, Wires, Rubber, Cords etc'; W H Briscoe & Co of 32/33 Cox Street, St Paul's Square, offered metal accessories, and Dunlop, of Manor Mills, Aston, advertised 'aeroplane fabric... carefully tested to withstand the effects of boisterous wind and inclement weather'. *Flight* on 9 October 1910 reported the formation of the Midland Aeroplane Co Ltd at 274 Corporation Street, with £2,000 capital - 'Manufacturers of and dealers in airships, aeroplanes, balloons, flying machines etc'.

Public enthusiasm for flying led to the inaugural meeting of the Midland Aero Club on 3 September 1909, at which a letter of support from Joseph Chamberlain was read. It was stated that several aircraft were being constructed and that half a dozen of them would be ready for trial within six months. A fund was launched to buy flying machines and other equipment. The club, whose address was 'The Bungalow, Stechford', was trying to persuade 'prominent aviators' to come to Birmingham.

Within weeks, the formation of the Birmingham Aero Model Club was announced. At its meeting on 17 September it stated that 'although they were quite in sympathy with the Midland Aero Club, they thought the subscription of one guinea was more than many working men could afford to pay'. The Aero Model Club claimed in October that its membership included 'some of the most skilled and learned men of the city' and that it planned a £50 fund with which to fit up a workshop.

Between 27 September and 7 October Maxfield's third aircraft managed to fly, at Castle Bromwich, attaining a height of fifty feet in one hop. It was later exhibited in Birmingham's Masonic Hall, in New Street (possibly later the Forum Cinema). The display was opened by Colonel Cody and a Civic dinner was held.

At its meeting on 13 October, the Midland Aero Club Chairman viewed with 'sympathy and interest' the formation of other clubs in Bir-

mingham, but expressed concern that a multiplication of societies with similar interests would result in 'waste of energy and talent'. Three papers were given at this meeting: 'Making and Testing an Aeroplane' by Maxfield, now a member of the Club's Council, 'Impressions of a Flight with Cody' by W Ivy-Rogers, who is credited by some with conceiving the Club (Ivy-Rogers' flight had lasted four minutes, causing one to wonder how long his description took); and one by a Wolverhampton member on constructing an aeroplane. Austen Chamberlain, Sir Gerald Muntz, Sir Benjamin Stone MP and Neville Chamberlain, then a JP, agreed to be Vice-Presidents. A balloon section was formed using two balloons lent by Lt Lemprière.

As this is the last time we hear of Maxfield, and because of his special place in Midland aviation history, it is appropriate to record what else is known of him. Alfred Pericles Maxfield was born in 1877 on the sailing ship *Pericles* (hence the name) during a monsoon on the Indian Ocean, en route for Australia. By the time his family returned to England there were five more members. Alfred set up his own engineering business at Gosta Green, about where the Delicia Cinema stood. After his successful flight the Midland Aero Club presented him with a specially-struck medal. There are three possible reasons why he gave up flying. First, that his father told him to; second, that he ran out of funds, and third - and the most likely - that his actress wife agreed to come off the stage, as Alfred wished, if he would stay on the ground. Other Maxfield projects included commercial advertising, for which he rented a room over a chemist's shop in Nechells Green, fitted an opaque screen in place of the window and beamed hand-painted slides on to it with a magic lantern. He also invented an early type of health sun lamp using an infra-red tube, a neon-type sign and an early form of permanent waving for hair. He retired in the early 1930s but came back to work as a safety officer for ICI. At the beginning of the 1939-45 war Maxfield was granted a licence to develop a mechanical respirator. Again, though, he lacked capital. After the war he retired to Rugby, where he died in his nineties. The Maxfields one child died in infancy.

The Midland Aero Club had sent a deputation to see the Mayor and Corporation of Sutton Coldfield with a view to using Sutton Park for flying. On 13 November nearly 3,000 spectators saw model aeroplanes being flown there. A full-sized glider was present, but its pilot, J H Else, failed to get it airborne. 'Several times the glider was run down the hill, but the velocity was not sufficient to lift it from the ground'. It was hoped that a flying meeting would be held at Sutton Park the following Easter.

The former head executive of the Wolseley Sheep-Shearing Company, one Herbert Austin, had in 1905 started a factory at Longbridge to make cars. In December 1909 Austin built an aircraft with an FN engine for a Rev J Swann of Liverpool. 'It jumped but never flew', recalled the Austin house magazine eight years later.

The Midland Aero Club continued to meet frequently during the winter. At a social gathering at the Grand Hotel on 29 October, 'cinematograph pictures' of Blériot's cross-Channel flight were shown. In November it was resolved to admit 'lady members', the first 250 paying 10s 6d (52½p) annual subscriptions. The first Annual Dinner, at the Grand on 11 December, was addressed by the Lord Mayor. He urged 'that the Midlands of all places should lead in the construction of flying machines, the district being so obviously well suited to such an industry'. By the end of 1909 the Club had 250 members. Major Baden-Powell, guest speaker on 25 February 1910, 'looked forward to the day when he could come down to Birmingham and go over one of the factories for the manufacture of aerial machines for military purposes', The Major could not have appreciated how quickly, and on what scale, his hopes would be realised.

But for some, talk was not enough. On 5 March the Secretary of the Birmingham Aero Club (the word Model had been dropped),

F A Thompson, wrote in *Flight*: 'As Birmingham's enthusiasts have unfortunately been so slow in constructing full-sized machines, and the fact that we have no flying men in this great mechanical city, have all served to stimulate the following. I have already suggested locally that those gentlemen, who can afford, will subscribe the necessary funds for an aeroplane, and entrust the construction with members of the Birmingham Aero Club'. From other sources we know that Thompson had been indentured as an apprentice designer and modeller in 1907. We shall encounter him again.

The Birmingham Aero Club planned to exhibit models and light petrol motors at the Edgbaston Botanical Gardens on 21 May, but the death of the King Edward VII caused the event to be postponed until 10 June.

The Midland Aero Club had learned the previous October that Dunstall Park racecourse, Wolverhampton, could be used for flying when not in use for meetings. It now revealed that an aviation meeting would be held there in June 1910, with prizes worth £3,500. How they were financed is unclear, but by May hangars were almost complete at Dunstall Park and had been let to Capt Dawes, Humber Ltd, Mr Lisle, Star Engineering Co, G Heath and Mr Ivy-Rogers. Lt Seddon RN was building his own hangar next to the other sheds.

ALF. P. MAXFIELD. *Birmingham's First Flying Man.*
Flights from Sept 27th to Oct 2nd at Castle Bromwich
Golf Links. 1909. *Masonic Hall, Birmm*

JONES.   **THE CLIPPER OF THE CLOUDS.**   BIRMINGHAM

A Midland Aviation Syndicate, formed to run the Dunstall Park meeting, was promised £4,000. The event, held from 27 June to 2 July, was to be the first all-British meeting for British flyers, and was expected to attract 300,000 people. By 10 May several flyers, some of them now legendary, had agreed to take part. They included the Hon C S Rolls (of Rolls-Royce fame), Capt Bertram Dickson (then the best-known Farman pilot in Britain), the Hon Maurice Egerton, Cecil Grace, James Radley (a well-known amateur builder), S F Cody, Lionel Mander, Mr Foley, J Holder of Edgbaston and Granville Bradshaw - who would fly a locally-built Star monoplane. Messrs Mander, Holder and Bradshaw were Club members intending to make their initial flying attempts at the meeting.

The hangars were finished by the end of May and in mid-June flying commenced. Capt Dawes' Blériot was badly damaged on 15 June when, having orbited the Park once and just passed over some trees, it swooped down and then shot up again, then fell sideways fifty feet. Dawes escaped unhurt. During the weeks before the Meeting, Bradshaw's Star, Holder's Humber and Dr Hand's Demoiselle took up residence.

On the opening day of the meeting Grace demonstrated a new Short biplane powered by a 40hp ENV water-cooled engine, designated the S.27. The aircraft was the basis for all further designs by Horace Short.

The Meeting included competitions for cross-country flying (the course was to Albrighton, then Cosford water-works, Tettenhall chimney stack and back - twenty-one miles), longest time airborne, carrying passengers, best Midlands machine, bomb throwing and figure flying. The organisers' decision to allow only pilots with certificates, or who were able to prove their ability to fly safely, disappointed Bradshaw, Holder and Mr Harthill of Wolverhampton. Capt Dawes managed to convince the organisers, though, and flew round the Park twice. (Bradshaw went on to design the unsuccessful ABC radial engine in World War One, and also motorcycles).

The weather during much of the week was gusty and several events had to be cancelled. Nevertheless *Flight* proclaimed, 'Unstinted credit is unquestionably due to the promoters of the Wolverhampton flying week...that unqualified success may attend their efforts must be the sincere wish of all those concerned with the future of aviation in this country'. But - such were the dangers of flying in those days - it was only a matter of days before one of the stars of the show, C S Rolls, met his death whilst performing at Bournemouth on 12 July.

Three aircraft remained at Dunstall Park after the meeting - Preventeau with a Humber, Bradshaw's Star and Holder's Blériot. The Blériot turned over the next week but Holder was unhurt. In one of the sheds, Lt John W Seddon's remarkable aircraft was nearing completion.

Above: A mysterious postcard (John Marks)
Below: Seddon's astonishing 'Mayfly' (Flight)

"Good heavens," said the chief designer, "you've built my doodles!"
The Mayfly, the first all-metal aircraft, built by Accles & Pollock of Oldbury, Birmingham, in 1910

The Seddon aircraft, called the *Mayfly*, tactfully described by *Flight* as 'most unusual', was a monstrosity that defied description - something out of an H G Wells fantasy. Strictly speaking, it was a tandem biplane (a principle which *Flight* noted had not yet received any practical trial) with main planes being (again, uniquely) braced by crossed hoops instead of the usual struts and ties. The front wing surfaces acted as elevators while the rear ones were simply for lift. This contraption had been designed by Seddon and Walter Hackett, Chairman of Accles and Pollock, and constructed by that firm at Oldbury. It was towed from there the twelve miles to Dunstall Park by horse. It had two New Engine Co engines of 65 hp each, driving Beedle-type propellers made of aluminium. It was supposed to carry five passengers as well as the pilot. The thing contained 2,000 feet of steel tubing and weighed about a ton - making it probably the heaviest aeroplane of that time.

The inevitable happened soon after it emerged for ground tests on 7 November - the (right) wheel axle gave way under the load. In April 1911 *Flight* reported that Seddon was preparing for another trial run. However, he had overstayed his leave from the Navy and had to return. Seddon eventually retired to Cheltenham, where he was still living in 1963. One report, in the *Sunday Mercury,* said the *Mayfly* was picked to pieces by souvenir hunters, while Marcus Langley in a lecture to the Royal Aeronautical Society on 'A History of Metal Aircraft Contruction' on 1 December 1969, said it ended up as scrap in a Hendon back garden.

Walter Hackett was Managing Director of Accles and Pollock for most of his professional life. In World War Two he invented a new method of producing sten-gun barrels. He died in 1964.

Back in Birmingham, the Midland Aero Club embarked on another series of lectures and began a search for another landing ground nearer the city. Ebenezer Parkes MP presided over the Annual Dinner at the Grand in December. The report of his speech is thought provoking: 'Germany and France were devoting infinitely more in resources of men and money towards this object (aviation) than we were, and he could not but come to the conclusion that we were behindhand. . . There had not been a first-class war between any of the great powers in Europe for a long time. If this country were suddenly to be engaged in war and was unprepared to meet attacks from the air, they would stand a bad chance of being able to effectually resist invasion. . .Birmingham, of course, ought to be a manufacturing centre for machines'. Grim pronouncements, uncannily similar to those of Churchill twenty years later.

Airport security, 1911 style. . . Grahame White's aircraft at Bournville. (John Marks)

Postcard of Grahame White addressing crowd at Bournville. The card was sent to Miss Millie Dawes of Wolverhampton from her friend Olive of Bournville, who wrote: 'Now I am sure you will like him on this photo better than either of those you have got. I think he looks so pleasant, not being aware of the fact that he is facing a camera, is more natural. This was taken nine minutes after he came to earth, April 17, 1911, after flying from London'. (John Marks)

At the close of 1910 the Midland Aero Club was amongst the largest aviation societies in Britain, with about 475 members.

Meanwhile, the Birmingham Aero Club was organising competitions to fly models across Edgbaston Reservoir - usually, it must be said, with disappointing results. When in January 1911 the club reviewed the previous year, it noted 'meagre financial support' and 'slow but solid progress'. Nevertheless it planned a second aviation exhibition, to be held at Bournville on 17 and 18 April. When in early April it was learned that Claude Grahame-White, probably the most famous aviator of the day, would open the exhibition, they never imagined that he would fly up from Hendon - surely he would simply catch a train. However, at 5.45 am on 17 April Grahame-White took off in his 50 hp Gnome-Farman and followed the railway from Harrow to Fenny Stratford, where thick mist forced him to land. It was 4.15 pm before he got airborne again. Grahame-White flew past Bletchley, Towcester and Dunchurch, near where he landed briefly to take on petrol. Finally he landed on a football field in Sparkhill to ask the direction of Bournville, where he touched down at 6.35 pm.

The other excitement of the Bournville meeting was that some of the models on display strayed on to the adjacent railway line.

By August the Birmingham Aero Club had made its headquarters on the Yardley Wood Road at King's Heath. 'The size of the field and the absence of trees mark this ground as a spot for future aviation meetings, or as an alighting spot for aviators coming to the Midlands from the South'.

Another pioneer came to Birmingham in March 1911 when Samuel F Cody lectured to the Midland Aero Club at the Grand. He said that 'although he thought the dirigible might prove of use in many directions, his faith was pinned to the aeroplane'.

A Short Brothers balloon made of Dunlop fabric graced the 1911 Olympia Show. 'On the Dunlop stand aviators' outfits are also con-spicuous, and amongst other garments will be found a leather combination suit, water-proof jackets and overalls, Harris tweeds, and caps to protect the entire head'. The Wolseley stand featured 60 and 120 hp engines, the latter available in versions for aircraft and dirigibles.

Lighter-than-air aviation was even more troubled by bad weather than winged flight. The balloon and airship pioneer E T Willows wanted to fly his airship from Watford to Wolverhampton in March 1911 but had to deflate it and take it by rail. After waiting at Dunstall Park for six or seven days for a gale to subside, he inflated his airship at the Knowles Works on Friday 31 March. It took ninety minutes to pump in 42,000 cu ft of hydrogen.

The next afternoon Willows ascended to fly over Birmingham, but between Walsall and Great Barr a feed pipe came adrift, so he landed in a field. His mechanic and Gilbert Dennison of the Midland Aero Club there helped to fix it. They then continued to Handsworth Wood, where they circled Dennison's house twice, and on to the city centre, where Willows flew round the Town Hall and Council House at between 600 and 900 feet, attracting a big crowd. The fifteen mile return journey to Dunstall Park took thirty-five minutes. In the evening and during the next afternoon Willows made several local flights with passengers, but windy weather on Monday ruled out further flights.

In September 1911 the Midland Aero Club launched a scheme whereby one could hire Lt Lemprière's balloon, which could carry three passengers, for twelve guineas. These trips would normally start from Dunstall Park, where a twelve inch gas main had been installed.

A 'Championship of the Midlands' for modellers was held by the Birmingham Aero Club at Billesley Farm on 7 October. 'A club aeroplane and permanent aerodrome at Billesley is being actively engineered', announced the club's press secretary. One of the many on-lookers at their meetings wrote to *Flight* (16 September 1911), 'At a recent meeting of the Birmingham Aero Club's flying ground at

Billesley Farm, King's Heath, a biplane glider of 37 ft span, and with pilot aboard, was towed by six men against a wind of about 30 miles an hour, and when they had attained a speed of 6 or 7 miles an hour the glider rose easily to a height of about 25 feet. Now it is obvious that a great deal of energy of the towers was taken up in moving themselves over the ground, and only a small amount left for raising the huge glider and pilot, and maintaining them in the air at an air speed of 37 miles an hour. In the face of this simple experiment, does it not seem that a large amount of the power on present-day aeroplanes must be running to waste. Where is the fault? The aero clubs should attempt to solve the problem. . .' By November the club had built a workshop and converted its glider into a biplane. A lamp and small coal stove were installed in the shed to facilitate work during the winter. One gets the impression from contemporary accounts that while the club was busy flying models and the glider each weekend, it was seen more as a hobby - early aspirations to be a 'proper' flying club seem to have faded.

During 1911 there were frequent advertisements for 'Vickers Duralumin - an alloy as strong as mild steel but only slightly heavier than aluminium - eminently suited for use in Aeroplane and Airship construction', made by the Electric and Ordnance Accessories Co Ltd (a Vickers subsidiary) at Aston. Wolseley continued to promote its 30 hp (four cylinder), 60 hp (eight cylinder) and 120 hp (eight cylinder) engines. A 60 hp V8 was used on the B.E.1 aircraft, which first flew on 4 December 1911, until 18 June 1912. In 1912 Archibald Graham Forsyth joined Wolseley to work on the design and construction of the aircraft. He joined the Royal Flying Corps in 1914 and was later Fairey's chief designer - he was responsible for the promising and revolutionary Rotodyne in the 1950s.

Two of Willows' balloons appeared over Birmingham city centre in October 1911. They were launched from the flat roof of Heath's garage in John Bright Street carrying advertising for the garage.

Flight on 11 November 1911 carried its first reference to an aerodrome being established on the playing fields at Castle Bromwich. Negotiations, it said, had been 'practically completed' between the Midland Aero Club and the Birmingham Playing Fields and Open Spaces Society and a hangar for Willows' dirigible had been erected. He was expected to fly over his City of Cardiff when the weather allowed. 'It is hoped, too, that one or two prominent aviators may be induced to make their headquarters at Castle Bromwich', By 23 March

1912 the negotiations to occupy the site had been completed and the Midland Aero Club was installing a glider and a 'mechanical trainer'.

In May The Aero magazine described Castle Bromwich: 'The aerodrome is about 1,100 yards long by 400 yards broad. The surface is decidedly good and very level. Originally the land was used for sewage farming, and little by little the surface has been laid on and carefully kept flat - sufficiently flat, indeed, to afford good cricket and football grounds, to which use in later years they have been put. Some fourteen feet below the surface various large culverts exist for the purpose of drainage. These serve to keep the ground in excellent condition; in fact, even after the heavy falls of rain and snow during January there was not the least trace of the formation of pools of water. The land is covered by grass and lies towards the middle of a large flat tract of considerable area and bounded by ranges of low hills. Once in the air, it should be possible to make circuits of from two to three miles in circumference, flying partly over the aerodrome itself and partly over the adjacent land, with the possibility of making an emergency landing at any point with perfect safety' . . . 'On the east side, at some distance from the back of the site of the hangars, is what may prove a great attraction to flying men, if one may judge from Brooklands, in the shape of a sewage farm in full operation'. The article confirmed that Willows was making Castle Bromwich his base; a two-seater dirigible was already kept in a shed there and the City of Cardiff was expected. It concluded, 'The flying ground itself is free from trees, with the exception of a low line bordering the Chester Road side and a few at the outer side of the north-east corner'.

As 1912 progressed the reports in Flight of activity at Billesley Common became more sparse, as did those of other model clubs. Perhaps the Editor had decided that events like the constitution of the Royal Flying Corps (13 April) and the consequent formation of squadrons, plus the daily excitements at Brooklands and Hendon, had first claim to coverage, and that modelling was no longer part of the mainstream development of aviation.

But one more reminder of the innocent, youthful fun of the Birmingham Aero Club comes from the report published on 23 March: 'Much excitement was caused by a person in scout uniform firing with a carbine across the aerodrome, one of the bullets going through a farm door a mile away. The culprit was caught and handed over to the police after an exciting four-mile chase'. The Boy's Own Paper would have been proud. As for the aerodrome site, in April 1916 the Midland School of Flying, King's 13

Heath, advertised a vacancy in *Flight* and in November 1919 Billesley aerodrome on the Yardley Wood Road was listed as being suitable for Avro 504Ks and similar aircraft. By the 1930s Billesley Farm itself was surrounded by housing.

In 1911 Bentfield C Hucks, former test pilot with Blackburns, flew his Blériot monoplane and gave passenger flights at the Castle Bromwich playing fields. The following year he flew from London to Birmingham and was sponsored by the *Daily Mail* to tour the Midlands, flying at public events. In 1913 he made some flights at the request of the Midland Aero Club from Dunstall Park. 'The amount of interest shown by Club members was very disappointing: the question of continuation of the Club, in view of lack of support, was under discussion, and for over a year its activities were very restricted', records a Club brochure, circa 1932.

Despite this, J C Savage, Huck's manager, challenged the well-known aviator Gustav Hamel to race Hucks and the *Birmingham Daily Post* offered a trophy and £500 a side. The race, on Saturday 30 August 1913, started at the Tally Ho grounds at Edgbaston and went via Redditch, Coventry, Nuneaton, Tamworth, Walsall and back via Quinton to Edgbaston. The original idea was for both men to fly 80hp Blériot two-seat monoplanes, but for some reason Hamel had to bring a 80hp Morane-Saulnier up from Hendon - a much faster machine.

His journey to the Midlands, incidentally, on 28 August, had taken ninety minutes including a stop at Nuneaton to check his position. Because the machines were unequal, the stakes were withdrawn and Hamel handicapped by taking his mechanic as passenger. Nevertheless, the race stimulated enormous interest and 30,000 people cheered them off. While Hucks and Hamel battled round the course, the Australian Sydney Pickles gave demonstration flights with a Blériot and Edwin Prosser flew his Caudron. (Austin's works magazine, *The Austin Advocate,* in April 1914 published a photo of Prosser passing over Longbridge in his 45hp Anzani-Caudron biplane on his way to give an exhibition flight at Northfield). Hamel won the race, but by only 20.4 seconds.

A few months later Benny Hucks was the first British pilot to loop the loop, on 27 November at Hendon. He returned to the Tally Ho grounds on 14 February 1914 to demonstrate his new trick before an audience of 20,000. By the time of his Birmingham demonstration he had looped 148 times; he looped another six times while back in Birmingham. When war came Hucks was called up for RFC service, but because of persistent pleurisy was eventually posted home for special duties. He then tested de Havilland aircraft. Hucks died in 1918 of pneumonia following influenza. He was, by all accounts, a much liked man.

Was it just coincidence that on the day of the Hucks-Hamel race the rival of the *Daily Post,* the *Illustrated Weekly Mercury,* had as its front-page headline, 'TO REVOLUTIONISE AVIATION - Birmingham Man Invents a Wonderful Hydroplane - Impossible to get killed'? The story was about a hydroplane powered by a 10hp one-cylinder engine constructed by the Belmont Aviation Company of Ladywood, run by F A Thompson of Edgbaston - earlier a moving force in Birmingham Aero Club - and Rupert E James. James was quoted extensively in this article and also one the following week. He seems to have had a way with words: 'we have solved the problem of automatic stability...I have made a special study of the action of large birds in flight and I notice that they exert themselves much less than is commonly supposed. And I have been at the pains of making an imitation pair of wings for use in the same manner as the real things. That means that, without the engines, it will be a simple matter to fly by an adroit manipulation of the wings by means of levers. And then, it is impossible to get killed on an aeroplane of this description. I would trust the stoutest man in the world, were he also the greatest idiot, alone in my hydroplane, and know he would not come to grief!'.

The aircraft's engine weighed only thirty-eight pounds and its cylinder had a bore of 70mm and a stroke of 70mm. James went on to explain why such a small engine was chosen. 'All we need is an engine to rise. Once up, if the machine is to be at all effective, it must fly. Propulsion by engine is not flight in its true sense. Even a paving stone will hurtle through the air given sufficient power behind it, but that is not flying'.

The hydroplane had been constructed by a deaf and dumb mechanic, Mr Pickering, and had a wing span of thrity-three feet and a fuselage sixteen feet long. Allegedly it was flown by James from a 'carefully preserved reservoir in the neighbourhood of Birmingham', with Thompson as passenger.

The *Illustrated Weekly Mercury* on 6 September confidently predicted: 'BIRMINGHAM AEROPLANE TO FLY THE ATLANTIC'. James now announced the intention to build an aircraft to compete in the 1914 £10,000 Trans-Atlantic Competition. It would have two pilots, dual controls, fly fully-laden at 80mph and cross the Atlantic in fifty hours, setting down in the sea four or five times to refuel from waiting boats. Its span would be fifty feet and its engine 160hp.

It is also known that in 1912 or 1913 the

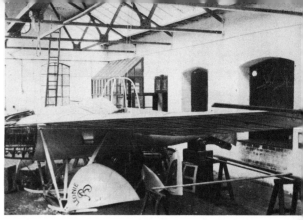

Levis company of Stechford was approached by James, who was designing an extremely light swept-wing tail-less aeroplane and wanted a 35 hp two-stroke engine which would turn a two-bladed propeller at 900 rpm. On this project, James was thought to be collaborating with or acting on behalf of Capt John W Dunne, who for some years had been experimenting with novel wing shapes and configurations. The aircraft was to be kept secret and built by three deaf-mute carpenters (Mr Pickering presumably one of them), It was to be called the *Mayfly* but, perhaps after somebody reminded James about the poor Seddon, was renamed *Leonie*. Dunne referred to this machine as D.9. Originally, it was planned to put floats on it and test it on Edgbaston Reservoir, but finally it received skids and wheels. The aircraft was taken to Castle Bromwich playing fields where, on take-off, a wing tip struck a goal post and it crashed, injuring the pilot's collarbone. The forlorn machine was taken back to the Levis factory and after the outbreak of war in 1914, dismantled. The engine was put in the works store in an old barn in Station Road. In 1953 a sharp-eyed visitor from the Science Museum in London, actually there to view a 1915 motor cycle engine, spotted the *Leonie* engine. The firm had it restored for exhibition at South Kensington, where it is today.

In mid-May 1914 Mr Raynham demonstrated 'water-planing' on Edgbaston Reservoir. On 20 June crowds flocked to Castle Bromwich to see competitors in the Hendon-Manchester-Hendon air race pass through, in both directions. Six competitors arrived and four continued to Manchester. The American W L Brock won the race. Grahame-White offered rides in his three-seat Farman.

And eight days later the heir to the Austrian Empire was shot in Sarajevo. . .

Top left: The fuselage of 'Leonie'. (A E Sinton)
Top right: 'Leonie' with wings attached. (A E Sinton)
Below: Claude Grahame-White demonstrating his Farman aircraft, Birmingham, 1914.

World War One

Soon after World War One began, in August 1914, Castle Bromwich was requisitioned by the War Office, which controlled the Royal Flying Corps. On 11 May 1915 No 5 Reserve Aeroplane Squadron was formed there, to use Maurice Farman Shorthorns and Longhorns. Its purpose was to provide the nucleus of a new squadron and train pilots. The unit became No 5 Training Squadron and left on 12 December 1917. No 34 Training Squadron, which had taken up residence at an earlier date, also moved from Castle Bromwich that month.

Nine other RFC and RAF squadrons resided at the airfield during and immediately after the war. Most of them were formed there before moving to operational bases. In chronological order, they were:

19 Squadron, formed on 1 September 1915 out of a nucleus supplied by No 5 Reserve Aeroplane Squadron. It trained at Castle Bromwich on Maurice Farmans, Avro 504s, Caudron G.IIIs and B.E.2Cs. It moved to Netheravon, Wilts, at the end of 1915.

34 Squadron, formed under Major J A Chamier with a nucleus from 19 Squadron on 7 January 1916. It used B.E.2Cs and moved to Beverley, Yorks, in March.

55 Squadron formed as a training unit on 27, April 1916. It operated B.E.2C, B.E.2E, F.K.8 and Avro 504 aircraft and moved to Lilbourne near Rugby on 10 June 1916.

54 Squadron, formed on 16 May 1916 under Capt E E Clark. It used B.E.2Cs from August, Avro 504s from September and later the Sopwith Pup. Initially its purpose was to defend Midlands industrial areas. It moved to London Colney, Herts, on 22 December 1916 before going to France.

38 Squadron re-formed on 14 July 1916 as a home defence squadron with some men from 54 Squadron. It operated B.E.2Cs, B.E.2Es, B.E.12s, possibly R.E.7s and, from September, F.E.2Bs. A site at Knowle was used by this squadron as a night landing ground. It moved to Melton Mowbray, Leicestershire, with effect from 1 October.

71 (Australian) Squadron, formed on 27 March 1917. It used various types, including the Sopwith Camel, and moved to France on 18 December. (On 19 January 1918 it became No 4 Squadron, Australian Flying Corps).

115 Squadron arrived from Netheravon on 17 July 1918. It received (locally made?) Handley Page O/400 night bombers that month and went to France in September.

132 Squadron re-formed at Castle Bromwich in October 1918 to fly D.H.9A day bombers but the formation was abandoned after the Armistice.

9 Squadron with no aircraft came to Castle Bromwich from Ludendorf on 31 July 1919. It was disbanded on 31 December.

Also, No 28 Reserve Squadron was here from June 1916 to July 1918. No 67 Reserve Squadron was formed in June 1917 and Nos 54, 55 and 74 in 1918. No 54 was the last Reserve Squadron to go, in July 1918.

Birmingham had the factories, the skills and the labour to make a key contribution to the equipping of the Royal Flying Corps, and later the Royal Air Force.

The supply of magnetos for aviation virtually ceased when war broke out because Robert Bosch of Germany was virtually the only supplier in bulk. Lucas bought the manufacturing side of Thomson-Bennett Ltd of Cheapside, Birmingham, which was making about two dozen magnetos a week and in December 1914 formed Thomson-Bennett (Magnetos) Ltd. Large numbers of French Gnome le Rhone aero engines used Thomson-Bennett hand starting magnetos. The firm moved into new seven-storey buildings in Great King Street in 1916. Later in the war bombers were fitted with two Lucas dynamos driven by eighteen-inch propellers fixed to the wing struts. These provided the aircraft lighting and warmed the crew's flying suits. A landing light system called the Orford Ness was made by Lucas, with four powerful lights fixed to the undercarriage. It was tried out on a Handley Page aircraft at Upavon. The cold storage room in the Birmingham Meat Market in Bradford Street was used to test, for use at high altitude and in the Arctic, a Lucas self-starter for a 240 hp 12-cylinder Sunbeam engine for seaplanes. (Immediately after the war, the Vimy in which Alcock and Brown flew the Atlantic used Lucas dynamos to power lamps, flares, horn, wireless and the heating of the airmen's clothes. The R34 that made the first double-crossing of the Atlantic used Lucas self-starters for its engines).

At Adderley Park, Wolseley Motors Ltd made nearly 4,500 engines and spares equivalent to another 1,500 units, plus nearly 700 aircraft, B.E.2Cs and 'Es and large numbers of S.E.5as. Also made were 850 wings and tailplanes and 6,000 propellers. On 22 March 1918 the Air Ministry announced that of a total of 274 German aircraft brought down in four weeks, 108 were attributed to Wolseley-engines S.E.5as. The

Wolseley W.4B Adder, used at one stage on the S.E.5a was a version of the Hispano-Suiza engine. By October 1918 all but two of the S.E.5a squadrons in France had aircraft powered by the 200 hp Wolseley Viper, a derivative of the Python. Wolseley would also have made 150 Sopwith Salamanders but the order was cancelled, at the end of the war.

The insatiable demand for war aircraft also led to the Austin Motor Co at Longbridge opening an aviation department. There was waste ground at the back of the Longbridge factory, to the south. It was too bumpy for flying, so early in the war Austin had the crown of the hill manually shaven off. It was an arduous task, possibly performed by German prisoners of war. This created a seventy-three acre, 4,500 foot diameter circular landing ground, used for test flying.

Austin had sacked six men in succession as head of his aircraft manufacturing department before, in late 1915, he hired twenty-three year old John Dudley North, formerly of the Grahame-White Company. With 100 men, many of them former crate-makers, North had to prepare for an initial order for R.E.7 biplanes. North later said, 'It was the worst design I had ever known'.

At the shareholders' meeting in early 1916 Austin announced that they had processed orders for goods other than cars worth £900,000 and had orders worth nearly £2 million. But, he promised, 'when the war is finished, there will be no difficulty in returning quickly to our regular business, or taking up any line that circumstances may warrant'. During World War One Longbridge's workforce grew from 2,800 to 20,000. (Today it is 14,000).

Towards the close of 1916 Capt Albert Ball, VC, DSO, MC, conceived the idea for a single-seat fighter, probably while he was working as an instructor in England. Ball, who was until 1914 an apprentice at Austins and whose father was a Director, persuaded the firm to take up the idea. J D North engaged C H Brooks to design the fighter. The belief that Ball actually designed this aeroplane has been proved to be mistaken.

By November 1916 the Government knew of the project and a specification was drawn up by 8 December. Austins reported in March 1917 that two machines were 'practically completed', but delays in finishing aspects of the design work hindered progress. A completed prototype went to Martlesham Heath for trials on 1 June, by which time Ball had been dead three weeks.

During the trials it was modified in many respects and finally obtained the serial number B9909 in October. It is doubtful, though, whether the aircraft ever displayed this marking. Engineless, it was put into storage at Ascot at the end of October 1917 and disappeared into obscurity. The second aircraft is thought not to have been completed.

The A.F.B.1, as it was known, was powered by a 200 hp water-cooled Hispano-Suiza V-8 engine. It was armed by two Lewis guns, one fixed on the upper wing and the other firing through the hollow propeller shaft. Its span was 30 feet, length 21 feet 6 inches and height 9 feet 3 inches. Empty, it weighed 1,426 lb and loaded 2,075 lb. It held 31½ gallons of fuel (not much, so as to improve performance). It could climb to 10,000 feet in ten minutes and had an endurance of two hours. At 10,000 feet it could fly at 126 mph.

North left Austins in 1917, having found his position under Austin untenable. He joined Boulton & Paul, for whom he supervised the design of such famous types as the Sidestrand and the Defiant, and mechanical aspects of the R101 airship. He was succeeded by John W Kenworthy BSc, who had previously supervised the design of the B.E.3, B.E.7 and F.E.8 aircraft. Kenworthy was accompanied by the mathematician H A Webb MA.

Kenworthy started by designing, with C H Brooks, the A.F.T.3 Osprey. This was a private venture (built under special licence no 17). It was a small single-seat fighter triplane built of wood with a fabric skin. The triplane configuration was an attempt to combine high performance with manouvrability and a good view. Its big propeller necessitated giving the Osprey's fuselage a high ground angle.

Various engines were tried: a 320 hp A.B.C. Dragonfly, a 230 hp Bentley B.R.2 rotary and a 110 hp Clerget 7D. The armament was two fixed, synchronised .303 Vickers machine guns and a movable .303 Lewis gun mounted on the rear spar of the cenre-section framework of the middle wing.

The Osprey's maximum speed at 10,000 feet - which could be attained in ten minutes twenty seconds - was 118 mph. Its endurance was three hours. Its empty weight was 1,106 lb and loaded it was 1,888 lb. The span was 23 feet and it was 17 feet 7 inches long.

Only one Osprey, serial X15, was built. It first flew at Castle Bromwich in February 1918 and was tested at Martlesham Heath in March. Work on two others, X16 and X17, was abandoned in March after the Sopwith Snipe was found to be superior.

A third disappointment lay in store for Austin with the Greyhound two-seat fighter-reconnaissance aircraft. It was designed by Kenworthy assisted by Harold Roxbee-Cox. The Greyhound was intended to succeed the Bristol Fighter, but the prototype was not finished until after the Armistice. This was at least partly due to trouble 17

Above: S.E.5a production at Longbridge, late 1918/early 1919. Most are in the batch E5637-5936, but F8014 (foreground) bears a US Air Service roundel. (BMIHT)
Below: S.E.5a F904, made by Wolseley, now flies with the Shuttleworth Collection. (S G Richards)

Above: R.E.7 production at Longbridge. (BMIHT)
Below: Handley Page O/400 J2258, made by the Birmingham and Midlands Carriage Co, is seen here with its wings folded. (via Roy Bonser)

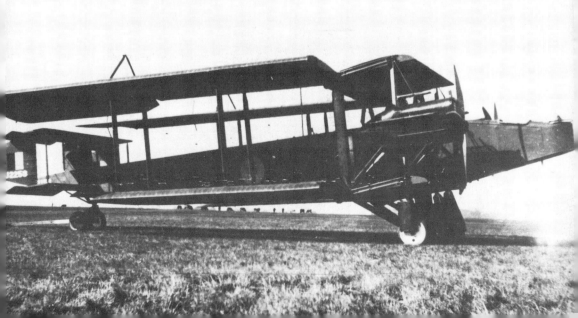

with the 320 hp A.B.C. Dragonfly 1 radial engine. The first Greyhound, H4317, went to Martlesham Heath for trials on 15 May 1919. Two others, H4318 and '9, were built and flown.

The Greyhound was armed by two fixed synchronised .303 Vickers guns and a .303 Lewis in the rear cockpit. Its maximum speed at 10,000 feet was 126 mph. It took ten minutes fifty seconds to reach that altitude. The empty weight was 1,838 lb and loaded 3,032 lb. The span was 39 feet and length was 26 feet 8½ inches.

During World War One the Austin company made about 2,000 aeroplanes - S.E.5as, R.E.7s and R.E.8s - and 2,500 engines. At peak production 350 engines a month were made. Production would have been higher had it not been for a strike in January 1918 by 10,000 workers, who were unhappy with their bonus scheme and irritated that as aircraft workers they did not receive a twelve per cent rise awarded to other munitions workers. They also thought their Works Committee chairman was being victimised.

The Birmingham & Midland Carriage Co built more than seventy Handley Page O/400 bombers at their Middlemore Road, Handsworth, factory and flew them from an aerodrome at Halford Lane, Smethwick. Not all of the aircraft ordered were completed and some became civil aircraft. The firm also made de Havilland D.H.10s.

A further 100 Handley Page O/400s were built by the Metropolitan Wagon & Finance Co in Birmingham.

Under Professor Lea at Birmingham University much research was done into the properties of light alloys of aluminium in aircraft and aero engines. Work on air flow, first for the Admiralty and later the Air Board, had to move to Farnborough because experimental facilities were lacking at the University, which during the war was primarily a hospital for wounded soldiers.

From 1 April 1918, the day the Royal Air Force was born, many of the aircraft made in Birmingham went first to No 14 Aircraft Acceptance Park at Castle Bromwich, which examined them and equipped them for operational use. Certainly many Austin-made S.E.5as and O/400s were checked there. At the end of the war the Acceptance Park had twenty-one storage sheds measuring 200 by 60 feet, two hangars measuring 280 by 150 feet, six measuring 210 by 65 feet and one of 170 by 80 feet.

Not surprisingly, Birmingham attracted the attention of the Germans and three airship attacks were made on the city. On the night of 31 January 1916 Zeppelins L19 and L21 bombed Birmingham, but the German's navigation was so erroneous that L21's commander, Kapitänleutnant Max Dietrich, thought he was bombing Liverpool and Birkenhead! L19 was commanded by Kapitänleutnant Odo Löwe, who believed he was over Sheffield. Most of their bombs fell in the Black Country and the suburbs. The Lord Mayor of Birmingham, Neville Chamberlain, made representations to the Government about the lack of warning of the raid.

On 19 October 1917, Zeppelin L42, commanded by Hauptmann Kuno Manger, dropped a bomb on the 'brilliantly lighted' Austin works at Longbridge, damaging the end of an outlying building, injuring two people. This attack caused the only fatality of the 'Zep' offensive against Birmingham - Dame Elizabeth Cadbury's pet monkey. A few bombs fell in other suburbs, not causing damage.

The third attack was on 12 April 1918, when L62, commanded by Manger, bombed Coventry and then passed over Hockley Heath on its way to Birmingham. It failed to inflict significant damage. According to a 1921 account, the airship 'turned tail immediately after crossing the city boundary, circled over Hall Green, dropped two big bombs in succession, the first on the Robin Hood Golf Course and the other on Manor Farm, Shirley, where they fell harmlessly into the fields, and the airship made a rapid retreat in the direction of Lapworth'. Manor Farm stood on the southern side of Olton Road at its junction with the Stratford Road, where today there is a parade of shops. Another local history states that at least some of L62's bombs fell in Olton Reservoir. Near Birmingham it was attacked by Lt C H Noble-Campbell of 38 Squadron, but the airship's defences were so vigorous that Noble-Campbell was wounded in the head and had to make a forced landing with his damaged aircraft.

On 10 June 1918 Birmingham's ground defences consisted of fourteen searchlights and fourteen 75 mm guns.

During 'Win the War' Week in September 1918, RAF aircraft dropped leaflets over Birmingham acknowledging the city's contribution to the equipping of the air force. They were entitled 'First Message from Mars'.

Above right: Bristol F.2b under construction at Longbridge (BMIHT)
Below right: Handley Page Transport's O/400 G-EAKG taking off. This aircraft was built by the Birmingham & Midlands Carriage Co and orginally was J2250 with the RAF. G-EAKG was operated until 1920. Many of the O/400s made in Birmingham later became airliners, one or two as far away as India. Another, G-EAMA made history by being involved in the first fatal accident involving a British scheduled air service.(British Airways)

Two Decades Of Peace

After the war, Austin retained a design staff which, under J W Kenworthy, produced a very small single-seat biplane, the Whippet. It has been reported that it first flew in 1918. The type was aimed at the private flyer with no facilities for complicated maintenance work. It had folding wings to enable it to be stored in a ten by twenty foot garage and be towed behind a car. A basic Whippet was shown at the 1920 Olympia Aero Show and received a good press. The advertised price was £450.

Alas, the Whippet was long before its time. The market was depressed by the economy and the huge numbers of ex-service machines available. The few examples that were built are listed in an appendix.

The Whippet was a robust machine, with a fabric-covered steel tubular fuselage with plywood decking around the cockpit. The wings were wooden with steel tube struts. There was a luggage compartment below the pilot's seat. Usually it was powered by a 45 hp Anzani six cylinder air-cooled radial that could be started from the cockpit. The span was 21 feet 6 inches and its length 16 feet 3 inches. Its maximum speed was 85-95 mph and the range 180 miles.

Roxbee-Cox again helped with the design. He later became Chief Calculator of the R101 airship design team, Director of the Royal Aircraft Establishment and Chairman of Power Jets (Research and Development) Ltd, which developed Whittle's jet engine, and was eventually to become Lord Kings-Norton.

The last Austin-designed aeroplane was the Kestrel, a biplane seating two, side-by-side. It was built for the 1920 Air Ministry competition and, flown by M D Nares, won third prize (£1,500) in the Small Aeroplane class. It was powered by a 160 hp Beardmore, had a span of 38 feet 6 inches and was 25 feet 6 inches long. It cruised at 83 mph.

The only Kestrel built was registered to Austin as G-EATR on 10 June 1920. It had a C of A from 7 August 1920 until 31 July 1921. It was put up for sale with spares in May 1924 and went to Fraser's Flying School, Kingsbury, London but was never used.

Despite its lack of commercial success, Austin's design team produced several engineers who would make their mark on British aviation. Apart from North and Roxbee-Cox, there was Joseph Smith (1898-1956), who served his apprenticeship at Longbridge. In 1921 Smith joined Supermarines as senior draughtsman, becoming Chief Draughtsman in 1926. He worked closely with R J Mitchell on the design of the Spitfire and after Mitchell's death was instrumental in the development of this classic fighter. J D Scott, in his history of Vickers, said 'If Mitchell was born to design the Spitfire, Joe Smith was born to defend and develop it'. Readers of the absorbing autobiography of Spitfire Chief Test Pilot Jeffrey Quill (*Spitfire: A Test Pilot's Story*) will find numerous references to how Smith ensured that the operational life of the Spitfire was extended well beyond the crucial summer of 1940 on into the great European offensive of 1943-45.

According to Lord Austin's daughter, the post-war production of aircraft was abandoned (in 1920) simply because it was too specialised and uneconomical.

Opposite: Austin Whippet K158 (BMIHT)
Below: The Austin Kestrel (Flight International)

A few engines were stored in the basement of the Longbridge North Works machine shops, probably to be melted down for the war effort after Austin died in 1941 (according to letter from F T Henry, *Aeroplane Monthly* April 1978). At least one Austin engine took to the air before aircraft production recommenced in the late 1930s, though - an 847 cc water-cooled Austin Seven engine, presumably modified, used on the Mignet H.M.14 Pou du Ciel ('Flying Flea') ultra-light aircraft G-AEEI.

The Cofton Hackett landing ground was used mostly in the 1920s and '30s as a test track for cars. On the weekend of 6/7 May 1929 Alan Cobham brought his 'circus' to what was described on the handbills as 'Northfield Aerodrome'. In connection with the visit a competition was held on 2 May to guess the height of a 'Mystery Plane' (described as a 'Siddeley Scout') over Birmingham. Sixty 10 shilling flight tickets were to be won, profits going to the Royal Cripples Hospital, Northfield. Cobham returned to Birmingham in September with his D.H.61 Giant Moth G-AAEV *Youth of Britain* at the end of his four-month tour to campaign for the development of municipal airports, during which thousands of council dignitaries were given flights. Cobham's 'circus' returned on 27 May 1932 to mark National Aviation Day. However, while on approach in his airliner with fifteen passengers on board, rain blurred his petrol gauge and forced him to land on Row Heath Recreation Ground, Bournville. The 'circus' came again to Cofton Hackett in May 1933. It is thought that in 1934 there was a Cierva demonstation on the landing ground and that in 1933/34 a flight of Hawker Harts landed.

CASTLE BROMWICH

With the return of peace, Castle Bromwich became a very quiet place indeed. Air services were sporadic and there was little private flying in the early 1920s. The RAF Air Historical Branch's version of the aerodrome's history says that soon after the war the site was almost used for housing, but the Air Ministry responded to pressure to retain it and licensed it as a civil field.

On 12 May 1919, twelve days after the resumption of civil flying, a Handley Page O/400 flown by Lt Col W Sholto-Douglas dropped newspapers by parachute at various points along the route London-Nottingham-Northampton-Lichfield-Birmingham (where he landed)-London.

The Air Board acquired Castle Bromwich in August 1919.

A twice-daily service from Hendon by British Aerial Transport Co is reported to have opened on 30 September, but although a BAT F.K.26 flew along the route the previous day, there is no evidence of later flights.

From 1 to 6 October, during the railway strike, the RAF flew mail and newspapers from London (Hounslow) to Birmingham. The surcharge was two shillings (10p) per ounce. Also during the strike, Vickers Ltd flew their mail between London and Birmingham and on to Sheffield and Barrow in the Avro 504K G-EADS piloted by L Jones.

In November, a de Havilland D.H.9 named 'City of Birmingham', paid for by residents of the city, was presented to South Africa at Castle Bromwich.

Handley Page Transport Ltd commenced an internal service from Cricklewood on 22 December 1920. The first flight was by R H McIntosh in a Handley Page O/11, either G-EASL or 'M or 'N.

Seventeen competitors in the first King's Cup Air Race stopped at Castle Bromwich on Friday 8 September 1922. On 13 July 1923 King's Cup competitors again passed through.

From 20 February to 2 March 1923 the Daimler Airway, operating D.H.34s, started to call at Castle Bromwich on it London-Manchester service, in order to serve the British Industries Fair. The first service was to have been the previous day, but bad weather prevented the aircraft from leaving Manchester. The British Industries Fair (BIF) was a forerunner of the National Exhibition Centre, run by the Birmingham Chamber of Commerce, opened in 1920 on just two acres south of the aerodrome.

On 15 September 1923 the de Havilland Aircraft Co Aeroplane Hire Service began a series of mail and dummy mail flights over the route Plymouth-Birmingham-Manchester-Belfast. This was on the recommendation of the Air Mail Committee and with the support of the Air Ministry, Plymouth Chamber of Commerce and the GPO. The flights, which were often hampered by bad weather, lasted for a month.

Below left: Avro 504K at Castle Bromwich. The aircraft is marked 'The Midland Aviation Co., Castle Bromwich'; we are fairly confident that it is G-EALE. (J S Beach)
Below right: Imperial Airways Handley Page W.9 Hampstead G-EBLE at Castle Bromwich. This aircraft served with Imperial Airways from March 1926 to January 1929. (Albert Turfrey)

The first run was by Alan Cobham in a D.H.50 with four passengers.

The *Birmingham Gazette* reported on 10 May 1924 that on the following Monday the newly formed Imperial Airways would operate its first 'home' service, in connection with the British Industries Fair. The first flight was to be piloted by Capt F L Bernard, Imperial's chief pilot.

In 1925 the Air Ministry fostered the formation of Light Aeroplane Clubs by offering each officially recognised club the gift of two de Havilland Moths and financial support for training civilians. The Midland Aero Club was the second to join the scheme, and decided to operate from Castle Bromwich. Flying was resumed when the first Moth was delivered in September 1925, when the Club had about twenty-five active flying members. The official re-opening was on 6 October.

On 16 July 1927 the Club organised the Birmingham Air Pageant, which was attended by 100,000.

The Air League Challenge race was held at Castle Bromwich that day as part of the Pageant. Norman Jones won it in the ANEC II G-EBJO, which flew to Woodford and back, 232 miles, at an average speed of 73.5 mph. The Pageant involved nearly 100 aircraft, including RAF Horsleys, a Siskin, a Hinaidi, some D.H.60s and Gamecocks of 32 Squadron. The Lord Mayor went up for a flight in the Armstrong Whitworth Argosy airliner G-EBLO *City of Birmingham*. Another successful Pageant was held on 9 June 1928. King's Cup competitors were to be seen again in 1928 (20 July) and 1929 (6 July).

The famous flyer Bert Hinkler flew in on 7 November 1927 in the Fokker F.VIIA G-EBTS *Princess Xenia*.

The Midland Aero Club's flying hours steadily grew from 411 in 1925 to 551 in 1927, 1,216 in 1928 and 1,360 in 1929. The economic recession and two poor summers caused the number of hours to drop to 1,142 and 1,105 in 1930 and '31 respectively. The Club's Chief Instructor from 1927 to 1929 was Tommy Rose, later a King's Cup winner.

The aerodrome was brought within the Birmingham City Boundary in 1931.

Above: Imperial Airways Argosy G-EBLO and a Gloster Gamecock at the 1927 Aerial Pageant, Castle Bromwich. (Flight International)

Right: A clearer view of the Lord Mayor's pleasure flight aircraft, Imperial Airways Argosy G-EBLO 'City of Birmingham' - the name is carried on the aircraft's nose. (via R Bonser)

Below: Aerial view of Castle Bromwich airfield. The aircraft is Handley Page W.8b G-EBBI, operated by Handley Page Transport from 1922 to 1924, then very briefly by Imperial. The Toro Soap Works, long a landmark, are beyond the track. The BIF sheds can also be seen. (M Butler)

Members of the Royal Family frequently passed through. The King and Queen arrived to visit the British Industries Fair on 23 February 1928. On 27 February 1934 the Prince of Wales visited the BIF, we think coming in Vickers Viastra G-ACCC, and came again in the King's Flight Dragon Rapide G-ACTT on 23 May 1935. On other occasions he was guest of 605 Squadron. Prime Minister Ramsay MacDonald arrived by road on 6 April 1934 and left by air for the inauguration of Midland and Scottish Air Ferries.

Many Brummies remember the airships that flew over the city at this time. The R101 spent more than half an hour over Birmingham on 18 October 1929 - classes of children were rushed outside to see it that sunny morning. It was in the district again the next day. Its sister ship the R100 flew over the city at night before its Canadian voyage, and the *Graf Zeppelin* flew over Birmingham on 3 July 1932. This was the last airship to be seen over the city for almost exactly forty years - the next was the Goodyear *Europa* on 5 July 1972.

It has been reported that a 'Castle Bromwich Flying Club' was active in the early 1930s.

On 16 June 1930, Imperial Airways used an Argosy to open a thrice-weekly London-Birmingham-Manchester-Liverpool route. The first southbound service was operated the next day with Argosy II G-AAEJ *City of Coventry*. The service was withdrawn on 20 September but is noteworthy because it was subsidised by the corporations of Birmingham, Liverpool and Manchester. Several reasons have been cited for its closure, including that the competition from the railways was too intense and that weather on the route made it overly unreliable.

In 1933 the Great Western Railway chartered the six-seat tri-motor Westland Wessex IV G-AAGW from Imperial and used it to operate from Plymouth to Torquay (Haldon aerodrome) and Cardiff. From Monday 22 May the route was extended to Birmingham and operated daily, leaving Castle Bromwich at 0930 and arriving at Plymouth at 1220. The return journey left Plymouth's Roborough aerodrome at 1600 and arrived at Castle Bromwich at 1850. The single fare from Birmingham to Plymouth was £3. The service was prompted by the railway's concern about airline competition, but it was too costly to run and closed on 30 September.

A service from Liverpool (Hooton) to Castle Bromwich was opened by Midland & Scottish Air Ferries in co-operation with Redditch Garages Ltd on 19 February 1934. A service to Heston also began on this date. Again, these services were in conjunction with the British Industries Fair. They were operated with Airspeed Ferry biplanes. The fares were London-Birmingham 32s 6d (£1.62½) single and 50s (£2.50) return, and Liverpool-Birmingham 30s (£1.50) and 45s (£2.25).

Above: Royal Dragon G-ACTT arrives at Castle Bromwich (Albert Turfrey)
Below: GWR's Wessex IV G-AAGW (R Bonser)

Above: Midland Aero Club Moth Majors G-ACNR and G-ACOG at Castle Bromwich.
Below: Castle Bromwich, about 1930. On the far right is the D.H.60 G-EBTH. It looks as though nine Wapitis are beginning their take-off run. The two aircraft nearest the camera are probably Avro 504Ks. (RAF Museum)

A twice-daily weekday service from London (Romford, later Abridge in Essex) to Birmingham and on to Liverpool and Glasgow was operated from 9 April to July 1934 by Midland & Scottish.

By the 1934 season Great Western Railway Air Services had become Railway Air Services, run by four railway companies and Imperial Airways. It was certainly intended to recommence services through Castle Bromwich on 30 April, from Plymouth and Cardiff and continuing on to Liverpool, but other authority has it that the first service was in fact on 7 May, using the D.H.84 Dragon G-ACPX. The Sunday journey was discontinued in 1934. A second RAS route opened on 30 July - a twice-daily Birmingham-Bristol (Whitchurch)-Southampton-Cowes service, using D.H.89s G-ACPP and 'R. The first flight on this summer service was, however, by D.H.84 G-ACPY. From 20 August RAS called in at Castle Bromwich on its Heston-Glasgow service, which was operated with the wireless-equipped D.H.86s G-ACVY and 'Z. Actual movements of 20 August were: Wessex G-AAGW (Capt W Armstrong) from London; Dragon G-ACPX from Liverpool and on to Cardiff, Haldon and Plymouth and return, and G-ACPY to Bristol and back. RAS also commenced carrying mail to Manchester from 20 August. The Glasgow service was withdrawn on 1 November.

By 1934 the Midland Aero Club was thriving again. Besides monthly dances, on 8 September it held a garden party and display to celebrate its twenty-fifth birthday. Thirty or so aircraft turned up and aerobatic displays were given by a Tomtit and a British Klemm Eagle. The RAF D.H.86 G-ACPL *Diana* and a brace of Dragons gave joy flights. During the afternoon various races and precision flying competitions were run.

Late in the afternoon on 9 December 1934 Club Moth G-ACOH, piloted by Frank Smith, collided with Hart K3887 of 605 Squadron, with Flg Off W C Barnaby and AC/2 F M Hardie on board. All three were killed. It appeared that both aircraft were coming in to land but the Hart's occupants failed to see the Moth, which was below and ahead, probably in a blind spot. The inquest passed a verdict of accidental death with no blame to be attached to either pilot.

MAC's flying hours grew from 1,405 in the year ended 31 March 1934 to 1,455 the following year. The Club's chief instructor at this time was Wilfred H Sutcliffe, who had joined in 1928 after eleven years in the RFC and RAF. He must have been busy, for in February 1935 the Air Ministry gave approval for the Club to give blind flying instruction, which commenced by May. Sutcliffe left the Club when war came in 1939 to join Rolls-Royce as a test pilot.

Club membership in 1935 cost £4-4s (£4.20). Dual instruction was charged at £2 an hour; solo cost £1-16s (£1.80) and blind instruction £2-10s (£2.50). 'Pupils with average ability', the Club advertised, 'can learn to fly and obtain their pilot's 'A' licence for approximately £25'.

Railway Air Services' operations at Castle Bromwich in 1935 were on a much more ambitious scale than before. The services to Croydon and Manchester (Barton) recommenced in April, followed on 27 May by a new route from Nottingham (Tollerton) and on to Cardiff, Denbury and Plymouth, operated by Dragons G-ADDI and 'J, and another from Liverpool and on to Bristol (Whitchurch), Southampton, Portsmouth and Shoreham (near Hove), using D.H.89s G-ACPP and 'R.

On a typical 1935 summer weekday the first scheduled arrivals at Castle Bromwich would be from Liverpool and Nottingham at 0935, which had left at 0900 and 0910 respectively. Ten minutes later they would be on their way to Bristol and Cardiff respectively, which they would reach at 1025 and 1045. At 1115 the service from Bristol would land, to leave for Liverpool ten minutes later. Close behind would be the plane from Cardiff at 1120, which at 1130 would depart for Nottingham. The daily southbound service from Manchester would arrive at 1210, to leave five minutes later for Croydon, where it would touch down at 1305. The northbound service from Croydon would be next, arriving at 1600 and again only staying on the ground for five minutes. At 1700 the second flight from Nottingham bound for Cardiff would pass through, followed five minutes later by the second Liverpool-Bristol service. Last movements of the day would be those from Bristol (arrival 1845, continuing to Liverpool at 1855) and Cardiff (arrival 1850, continuing to Nottingham at 1900).

In early 1935 two Birmingham brothers, Alfred and John Ellison (John later owned Hornet Moth G-AFDF, seen in a pre-war photo at Elmdon, parked outside Midland Aero Club entrance), won and came second in two races at the Morocco International Air Rally. On Saturday 20 July the Midland Aero Club held a 170-mile 'Contact' race to Stoke (Meir), Nottingham (Tollerton), Leicester (Braunstone) and Northampton (Sywell). The Club's publicity officer enthused in *Flight,* 'Pilots must land at each of these control points and hand in their race card for a signature before taking off into wind. There will be some glorious 'swish-tail' approaches and some riotously fast taxying at the control points!' But *Contact,* the club's magazine, said after the event that 'such procedure was conspicuous by its absence'.

Despite poor weather, the event was well attended. Alex Henshaw, flying an Arrow Active, won the sealed time arrival competition. Then the nine Contact race competitors left. Listed by handicapped time of departure, they were:

15.00:00	G-ABAL Gipsy Moth (pilot J L Cave)
15.06:38	G-AAII Genet IIIA Martlet (pilot A W Tweddle)
15.06:44	G-ACTN Cirrus IIIA Hawk (pilot H W Badger of the North Staffs Club)
15.08:30	G-ACHW Genet Major Avro (pilot Miss E A Tyzack of Northants club)
15.12:39	G-ACJF Monospar (pilot G S Davison, Castle Bromwich)
15.18:17	G-AAIG Hendy Hobo (pilot Flt Lt R Duncanson, entered by Lord Crichton-Stewart)
15.23:48	G-ABYU Puss Moth (pilot H L Johnson, Castle Bromwich)
15.24:00	G-ABIX Arrow Active (pilot Alex Henshaw)
15.31:01	G-ADAW Hawk Major (pilot Miss Ruth Fontes of the Reading Flying Club)

Opposite: Railway Air Services D.H.86 G-ACVY 'Mercury' takes on passengers at Castle Bromwich. (Albert Turfrey)

Below: de Havilland Cirrus Moth G-EBTH with wings folded, inside a hangar at Castle Bromwich. It was based from about 1928 and kept in a hangar next to the Toro Soap Works. It eventually moved to Elmdon in 1939. (via John Nicholds)

605 Squadron then displayed their Harts, Capt W Percival rocketed about in the Gull he had recently taken to Oran, then R A C Brie demonstrated the Autogyro. R A Duncanson in his Hobo was first back in the Contact race, averaging 98.75 mph. Incidentally, the Club President at this time was Gilbert Dennison, who we last traced (referred to as a Major) at the Banquet the evening before Elmdon was formally opened.

A frequent user of Castle Bromwich that summer was the Midland Gliding Club, which started flying at Handsworth on 26 December 1934. It initially used a Prufling and a privately-owned Falcon. By May 1935 it had forty-nine members. Its first visit to Castle Bromwich was on Jubilee Day 1935.

In 1936 Railway Air Services re-opened for business on 25 May, offering this season a Liverpool - Birmingham - Bristol - Southampton - Ryde-Shoreham service, with request stops at Meir for Stoke and Staverton for Gloucester. The Plymouth service was dropped. In July 1936 Norman Edgar (Western Airways) Ltd opened a service to Weston-super-Mare.

Another 'Contact' race was organised by the Midland Aero Club on 22 August 1936, using the same landing points but not Nottingham. Alex Henshaw has described this particular event (*Vintage Aircraft* no 13), 'To fly an aircraft at maximum speed right up to the point of landing and endeavour to throw off excess speed to land as near to the Marshall as you dared called for an exercise in flying - if you could call it that - which would have present day Air Traffic Controllers collapsing on the floor. To watch normally sedate pilots rushing to their aircraft, taxying with their tails up and ground staff ducking and rushing out of the way as competing machines tore along to the take-off lane to get off in the shortest time was a sight worthy of the Keystone Cops at their best'.

By the winter of 1936/37 at least some of the routes through Birmingham were available all year round. Subject to twenty-four hours notice, Railway Air Services' flights from Croydon to Liverpool, Belfast and Glasgow would call at Castle Bromwich to pick up or set down travellers.

On 1 July 1937 No 14 Elementary and Reserve Flying Training School opened at Castle Bromwich, operated by Airwork Ltd and using six Tiger Moths. During its early stages the School is known to have had Hawker Harts K3843 and K3902 (which hit wires landing at Castle Bromwich on 24 July 1938).

Railway Air Services operated two routes through Castle Bromwich during the summer of 1938: Croydon-Castle Bromwich-Stoke (on demand) - Manchester - Liverpool - Isle of Man - Belfast - Glasgow, twice daily on weekdays, and Manchester-Liverpool-Castle Bromwich-Staverton-Bristol-Southampton-Ryde-Shoreham, daily on weekdays. Until 25 June the Manchester flights used Barton but from 27th switched to the new Ringway airport. It is known that G-ACPR, 'EFH and 'EWR were the most common aircraft on the Manchester-Birmingham sector that summer.

The Midland Aero Club became associated with the Civil Air Guard in 1938, and gave instruction under that scheme.

In 1939 Great Western & Southern Airlines Ltd, formed in December 1938, took over the Railway Air Services routes previously sponsored by the Great Western Railway and the Southern Railway.

D.H.86B G-AEWR 'Venus' of Railway Air Services at Castle Bromwich. Delivered in summer 1937, it was lost during the evacuation of France in June 1940. (D C Crocker)

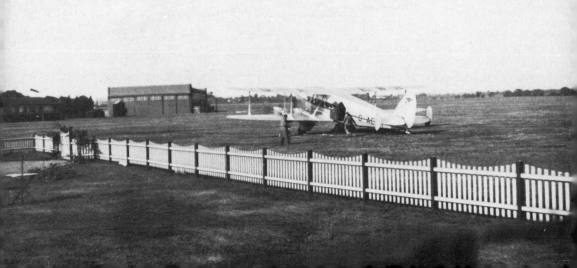

605 (COUNTY OF WARWICK) SQUADRON

No 605 Auxiliary Air Force Squadron was formed at Castle Bromwich as a day bomber unit on 5 October 1926, under the command of Sqn Ldr J A C Wright, DL, with Flt Lt F O Soden DFC as Adjutant and Flying Instructor. Its first aircraft, the D.H.9A E8686, arrived by air from Henlow on 25 October. Avro 504K and 504N aircraft were also delivered in 1926, but the D.H.9A remained the principal squadron type until 1930.

Flt Lt W R Cox MC, AFC, arrived to be Adjutant-Instructor on 12 May 1927 and in June the squadron held its first weekend camp. It contributed to the Birmingham Air Pageant on 16 July and left for its first annual camp, at Manston in Kent, on 31st.

On 22 August the squadron learned that it had won the Esher Trophy for its efficiency. This Trophy was presented to the Auxiliary Squadron displaying the greatest all-round efficiency, in subjects including bomb aiming, air navigation, photography and air gunnery. 605 was to win the Trophy six times in ten years - it was also successful in 1930, 1931, 1933, 1934 and 1935.

Squadron records state that during the summer of 1927 Fairey Fawns were flown to Glasgow on a navigational exercise, but it is not clear whether they actually belonged to the unit. The British Union of Fascists leader, Sir Oswald Mosley, lunched with the squadron that year.

Above: 605 Squadron's dual control Wapiti Mk. VI, K2237. (Albert Turfrey)

Below: Three Lynx-powered Avro 504Ns of 605 Squadron at the 1927 Air Pageant bomb an Eastern Castle Bromwich. (Flight International)

Ten aircraft each of 56 and 111 Squadrons, seven of 25 Squadron and a 32 Squadron aircraft were refuelled by 605 Squadron men at Castle Bromwich on their way to the Blackpool Air Display on 4 July 1928. Four Hyderabads staged through en route for Aldergrove, Northern Ireland, arriving on 5 July and leaving the next day.

Flt Lt S D Macdonald DFC became Adjutant in 1929. His assistant, who also joined 605 that year, was Flying Officer G W Tuttle, later an Air Marshal. On 20 February 1930 the first Westland Wapitis were delivered; the last D.H.9A left in June. Sqn Ldr Wright was awarded the AFC and qualified for the Territorial Decoration in 1931. HRH The Prince of Wales and HRH The Duke of York visited the squadron on 9 May 1931. When the Prince of Wales returned on 29 June he used the occasion to present 605 with the Esher Trophy. His visit to the British Industries Fair on 27 February 1934 was another chance to visit the squadron.

605 Squadron took part in the 'low bombing' event of the June 1933 Hendon Pageant, and also participated in the 1935 display.

In October the first Hawker Hart arrived, eclipsing the Wapitis by December. Some 10,438 people attended the Empire Air Display at Castle Bromwich on 25 May 1935. Lord Willoughby de Broke took over from Wright as Commanding Officer in March 1936. (Wright became active in local politics and was later Unionist MP for Erdington). Only 6,200 attended the Empire Air Display that year, which featured a Fury and two Bulldogs of the Central Flying School, a Heyford from Boscombe Down and a Sidestrand from Bicester.

Hawker Hinds arrived in August 1936 to replace the Harts, the week after 605 returned from its Annual Camp, held this year at Aldergrove, Northern Ireland. The 1937 Empire Air Day display was attended by 12,000. This year's highlights were a Harrow, a Blenheim, Anson and three Gladiators.

In early 1937 it was decided to spend £250,000 on Castle Bromwich over the next two years, building a big 'C'-type hangar and a new Headquarters for 605 Squadron.

The 1938 Empire Air Display was attended by 19,500, despite poor weather. In September, when the Munich crisis was at its height, 605 Squadron formed a mobilisation pool to receive, ration and house 1,000 reservists. 1,500 gas respirators were assembled in 13½ hours. The crisis diminished, though, and the squadron returned to normal in early October.

The unit was redesignated a fighter unit from 1 January 1939. The airfield was extended by 213 acres in anticipation of Hurricanes arriving. Gloster Gladiator I and II aircraft were received in February. Having just returned from camp at Tangmere, 605 returned there on 27 August with six Hurricanes, ten Gladiators and two dual-control Fairey Battles on strength, as international tension mounted.

Most of the subsequent history of 605 Squadron falls outside the scope of this book. Suffice to say it fought valiantly in the Battle of Britain. It was based at Baginton, Coventry, for a spell in 1941. During this time it flew a sweep over Birmingham on 4 August and damaged a lone Junkers Ju 88 carrying out a reconnaissance over the city on 30 August - the bomber later crash-landed in Eire. On 26 September 1941 the Squadron organised a flypast for Winston Churchill at the Armstrong Whitworth factory at Coventry where Whitley bombers were made and later in the day escorted the Prime Minister to Castle Bromwich.

On 31 October 1941 the Squadron left for the Far East but in early 1942 was captured by the Japanese.

A new squadron was formed in June 1942 and again in June 1946 a fresh 605 Auxiliary unit was formed, at Honiley. The colour this squadron received on 11 March 1954 and which hung in a Warwick church until March 1957, when all Auxiliary squadrons were disbanded, has returned to Castle Bromwich, though. On 23 September 1973 it was laid up in St Cuthbert's Church on the Castle Vale estate, on the site of the old aerodrome.

At least four visiting pre-war military aircraft met untimely ends at or near Castle Bromwich: a Martinsyde (Sqn Ldr Jones DFC) crashed on take-off on 20 July 1928; Hawker Audax K3710 of 77 Squadron crashed on landing on 23 August 1937 and Fairey Battle K7564 of 63 Squadron overshot whilst landing on 9 May 1938. Also, on 5 October 1928, a Bristol Fighter (Flt Lt Blackford) crashed 1½ miles south of the aerodrome in poor visibility. The pilot was unhurt and his passenger only slightly injured.

Top: Wapiti K1367 of 605 Squadron engineless in a Castle Bromwich hangar. (Albert Turfrey)

Middle: Hawker Hart trainer K3147 of 600 Squadron during a visit to Castle Bromwich. (Albert Turfrey)

Bottom: Westland Wallace at Castle Bromwich. This view clearly shows the unusual cockpit arrangement. The forward position has a sliding canopy while the rear hood is made of transparent segments that could be locked together to enclose the rear gunner or folded back to give his Lewis gun a clear field of fire. (A Turfrey)

Top: Hawker Fury K2037 of No 1 Squadron at Castle Bromwich. (Albert Turfrey)

Left: The Prince of Wales (the future King Edward VIII) arrives at Castle Bromwich in a Vickers Viastra G-ACCC. The Prince is talking to Sqn Ldr Cecil Wright of 605 Squadron. (Albert Turfrey).

Below: Siskins of 56 Squadron at Castle Bromwich. From left to right: J7160, J8971, J8647, J9879, J8948. (M Butler)

Opposite page:
Top: 605 Squadron's Hawker Hind K5539 during rehearsals for Empire Air Day, March 1938. (via M Butler)

Right: 605 Squadron's emergency vehicles. (Albert Turfrey)

Below: A two-seat training example of Sydney Camm's classic creation, the Hawker Hart, at Castle Bromwich. (Albert Turfrey)

A New Airport

In February 1928 Birmingham City Council instructed its General Purposes Committee to 'consider the possibility of establishing a municipal aerodrome. . . so that much of the continental traffic might be diverted from London to Birmingham direct, thereby stimulating the present and future trade of the city'.

After consulting the Air Ministry and Sir Alan Cobham, the City Engineer recommended in 1930 that the new airport should be at Longmore Road, Shirley. The cost would be £70,000. The council failed to reach agreement with the owners of the land, though, and sought compulsory purchase orders, but then the Engineer changed his mind, largely because of the rapid housing development in Shirley, and decided that Elmdon would be a preferable site.

A scheme to build the airport specifically as a means of reducing unemployment was put to the Government but shelved because of the economy cuts of September 1931.

The Elmdon project was revived in 1934 after the Air Ministry hinted that Castle Bromwich could not be used indefinitely as a civil airport. Originally the new airport was planned to occupy 300 acres, but the Council decided that this would now been inadequate and issued compulsory purchase orders for a further 200 acres. Parliamentary approval to divert various footpaths was secured and the purchase of the entire site financed by a Government loan.

In October 1934 a council deputation visited Heston and Croydon to inspect the layout and organisation. Also that month, enquiries were made into the possibility of linking the airport with Marston Green Railway Station. An Airport Committee was formed in November. Some of its members made a tour of European airports, including Amsterdam, Berlin, Copenhagen, Brussels and Hamburg, in April 1935. It was probably during this trip that Berlin Tempelhof Airport's design, with its canopies over the apron, were seen - later to be incorporated into the design of Elmdon's terminal. In 1938 Leonard Faulkner, who had been Clerk to the Airport Committee since its inception, and Alderman Charles Simpson, visited Berlin, Bremen and Hannover.

The Parliamentary Bill enabling Birmingham to build and operate a municipal airport, in 1935, included a clause allowing the Council to operate its own aircraft. This clause was reluctantly withdrawn after the Council was advised that it would meet considerable opposition.

In October 1935 Bickenhill Parish Council, in whose domain the airport was to be built, protested against the whole scheme. The Maybury report on the future development of British civil aviation, in 1937, also caused dismay, by not even mentioning Birmingham's role.

Final council approval for the new airport came on 4 February 1936. The cost was to be £½ million and it was proposed to have an electric railway and monorail link to the city centre, but the cost caused these ideas to be abandoned.

Construction work, by B Sunley & Co Ltd, began immediately. Fields were amalgamated by the removal of hedges, hundreds of trees felled, many ponds filled in, forty miles of drains

Opposite page:
Top: The architect's first design for the terminal building at Elmdon. (Airport Collection)
Middle: How the airport looked the day Leonard Faulkner was appointed Manager - 23 February 1939. (Airport Collection)

Bottom: Construction work proceding well, 24 March 1939. (Airport Collection)

Below: How the land at Elmdon looked before the builders moved in. (Birmingham Post & Mail)

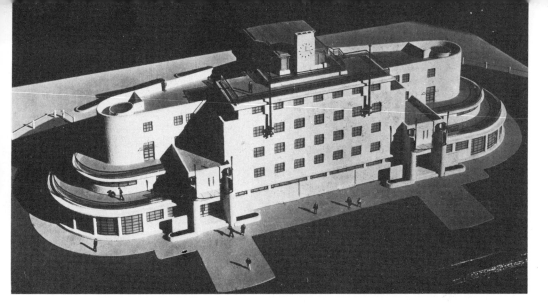

37

The signpost image contains the following text:

BIRMINGHAM AIR PORT

N W
S E

MANCHESTER (RINGWAY)

OSLO (FORNEBU)
713 m

BERLIN (TEMPELHOF)
VIA AMSTERDAM
641 m   1030 km

STOCKHOLM (BROMMA)
VIA HAMBURG
994 m   1600 km

AMSTERDAM (SCHIPOL)
277 m   445 km

BRUSSELS (HAREN)
286 m   460 km

ROME (ROMA LITTORIO)
VIA TURIN
992 m   1590 km

LONDON (HESTON)
88 m   142 km

PARIS (LE BOURGET)
                   487 m

NEW YORK
(FLOYD BENNETT FIELD)
3518 m   5660 km

NEWFOUNDLAND
2327 m   3740 km

DUBLIN (BALDONNELL)
205 m   330 km

BELFAST
VIA LIVERPOOL
228 m   367 km

GLASGOW RENFREW
259 m   417 km

Above: The signpost that was for many years a landmark at the airport entrance. There are plans to refurbish this lovely reminder of days past and display it in the new terminal.
Below: Elmdon's first air transport movement: the Dragon 'Volunteer', 1 May 1939.
(Birmingham Post & Mail)

laid and the top soil (of solid clay) removed and re-spread. The reinforced structure of the terminal building was designed and made by Holst & Co. The canopies each extended fifty feet out from the building, which itself was sixty-four feet wide. The architects, Norman and Dawburn, were particular proud of this feature.

On 23 February 1939 Leonard Faulkner was appointed Airport Manager with the then handsome salary of £650 per annum.

The first aircraft landed at Elmdon on 20 March 1939 when Whitney Straight arrived in Western Airways' D.H.90 Dragonfly G-AEDH to announce that his company would serve Elmdon from 17 June. From that date a thrice-daily Weston-super-Mare - Bristol - Birmingham - Manchester service operated, using G-AEDH plus the Rapides G-ACTU and 'FSO and the Percival Q.6s G-AFIX and 'FVU. The route attracted few customers though.

Elmdon opened for business on 1 May 1939, having cost £360,000. At this stage only 215 of the 800 acres by now available were in use, giving three grass runs of about 3,000 feet and a fourth of about 4,700 feet. Plans were being made for the Air Ministry to install a Lorenz blind landing system.

The ground floor of the terminal was occupied by the airlines and the Midland Aero Club; the second by administrative departments and the restaurant, while the meteorological, control and radio rooms were on the third.

The first arrival that grey, overcast morning was the two-seat Swallow G-ACXE from Castle Bromwich, piloted by Councillor H S Goodby of the Airport Committee, who had been flying since 1932, and who owned the Swallow jointly with his brother. The Lord Mayor, Alderman James Crump, was passenger.

The first scheduled arrival on 1 May was a Dragon Rapide named *Volunteer* of Great

Above: HRH The Duchess of Kent at the official opening of Elmdon, 8 July 1939.

Right: Judging by the planks and scaffolding around the terminal, this view was taken early in the summer of 1939. The wing foreground is of an Audax, no doubt of 44 E&RFTS.

Below: In this aerial view of Elmdon, taken in 1939, the Midland Aero Club Tiger Moth G-AFNU and three RAF Magisters can be seen. (via John Marks)

Western & Southern Airlines. It had left Liverpool at 0855 and, flying via Manchester, arrived at Elmdon at 0955. A few minutes later it left for Bristol, Southampton, Ryde and Shoreham. As it departed the Railway Air Services D.H.86 G-AEFH *Neptune* arrived from Croydon, en route for Liverpool, Belfast and Glasgow. These were, until 17 June, the only routes to operate through Elmdon.

Also on 1 May, the RAF's No 44 Elementary and Reserve Flying Training School was opened at Elmdon, operated by Airwork Ltd. Hawker Hind K5506, Hawker Audax K2024 and the Miles Magisters N3962, N3963 and N3965 are known to have served with this School, which operated only until the outbreak of war.

The ceremonial opening of the new airport was on Saturday 8 July. It rained torrentially for most of the day, causing the Airport Committee Chairman, Alderman A H James, to say to the *Evening Despatch* reporter, 'This weather is spoiling everything. I could cry'.

Air Minister Sir Kingsley Wood arrived in an Air Council D.H.86 (L7596 or N6246) just before noon, to be taken by the despairing Alderman James to the Civic Lunch at the Council House. Meanwhile Wing Commander J A Cecil Wright of the Airport Committee hosted sixty guests at a lunch in the terminal building.

The cloud base, as low as 300 feet at times, prevented Spitfires coming from Hucknall and only about half a dozen out of the 100 expected private aircraft turned up. One of those who braved the weather was Alex Henshaw, whose Vega Gull won the Concours d'Elegance for the best kept aircraft with the most interesting history.

After unveiling a plaque above the entrance to the terminal, the Duchess of Kent declared the airport open. The Prime Minister, Neville Chamberlain, was also there. *Flight* reported his speech: 'Events had made it necessary recently to concentrate rather on Royal Air Force expansion than on the development of civil aviation. In consequence, our Air Force was, in many ways, the finest in the world. Nevertheless, those who had been responsible for Birmingham's new airport had planned wisely for the future. He had no doubt that, if and when we emerged from the present condition of international tension, there would be an unprecedented development in civil aviation'.

The air display started with R A C Brie demonstrating a C.40 Autogyro. Then Fleet Air Arm Skuas took off and gave a limited display. The Piper J-4A Cub Coupe was the only other civil aircraft demonstrated. Eight Spitfires of an unnamed squadron then flew, followed by a Blenheim, a Lysander, after which 605 Squadron left for Castle Bromwich. There were then displays by a Whitley, a Hampden, a Blenheim, a Hurricane and a Bombay.

The Imperial Airways A.W.27 Ensign G-ADSW commanded by Capt Perry, was to have taken members of the Corporation for a flight but instead returned to Croydon.

Other visitors included the prototype D.H.95 Flamingo G-AFUE, on loan to Jersey Airways Ltd, and the Royal Flight Envoy G-AEXX, which earlier had taken the Duchess of Kent to Walsall. Western Airways offered joy flights in their new D.H.86 G-AETM and three Rapides, a Dragonfly and a Dragon, and Olley Air Services also offered joy flights.

The first visit by a foreign commercial aircraft and, we think, the only pre-war one, was by KLM's Douglas DC-3 PH-ASR en route from Amsterdam for Manchester and Liverpool on 2 July.

In late August, just a week before war was declared, Great Western & Southern Air Lines received proof copies of their proposed 1939/40 winter timetable, which included a daily Liverpool-Manchester-Birmingham-Bristol-Ryde (on demand)- Shoreham service and two flights daily to Croydon and Manchester (and on to Liverpool and Belfast), all commencing on 18 September. Plans were also made to operate the D.H.95 Flamingo from Liverpool via Birmingham to Shoreham and Paris, but this too never materialised.

The threat of war also ruled out the staging at Elmdon of the King's Cup Air Race and the Wakefield Trophy on Saturday 2 September. The Royal Aero Club called them off on 24 August, because many competitors were in the RAF or the reserves, handicappers and other officials had been called for duty, and service training at Elmdon and Castle Bromwich could not be interrupted.

Opposite page:

Above: A view of the terminal building taken from inside the nearest hangar, 1939. On the left is D.H.87B Hornet Moth G-ADKV, on the right D.H.80A Puss Moth G-AAZP. (Airport Collection)

Below: Western Airways Percival Q.6 G-AFIX seen at Elmdon in 1939 operating the short-lived and poorly supported thrice-daily Weston-super Mare - Bristol - Birmingham - Manchester service. (via N Doyle)

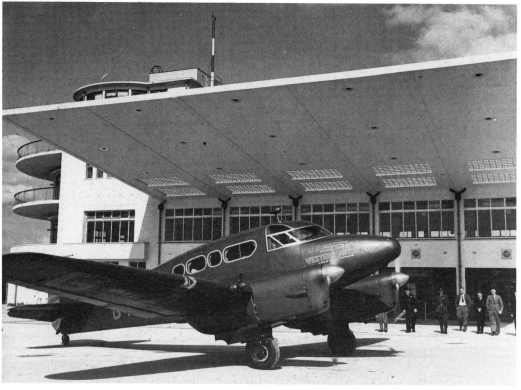

41

Preparation For War

During the winter of 1935/36, the European military situation and British attitudes to it changed dramatically. The failure of the League of Nations to intervene in the brutal Italian conquest of Abyssinia, and the German denunciation of the Treaty of Locarno and occupation of the de-militarised zone of the Rhineland signalled the end of collective peace-keeping.

The Royal Air Force was totally unprepared for European war. British aircraft manufacturers could not contemplate the scale of production that was needed, quickly, to achieve air parity with France or Germany. Consequently, the Air Minister, Viscount Swinton (formerly Sir Philip Cunliffe-Lister) announced, in April 1936, the 'shadow factory' scheme. Under this, the Government negotiated with the big car manufacturers to use their massive production potential. The State would give financial help towards the construction and equipment of these 'shadow factories', as well as production management. It did not escape those who heeded Stanley Baldwin's warning of 1932 that 'the bomber will always get through' that these new plants would help to disperse production.

Five car firms constituted the pre-war backbone of the scheme: Austin at Longbridge; Rootes Securities (which controlled Humber) at Coventry and Speke in Liverpool; Rover in Birmingham and Standard and Daimler in Coventry. Initially, all five produced components for the Bristol Mercury radial engine, which powered the Bristol Blenheim, Gloster Gladiator and Westland Lysander.

The early negotiations and preparations for shadow production at Longbridge took place between February and November 1936. Bromsgrove Rural District Council approved plans for a factory on twenty-three acres of land bought from farmers at Grovesley Lane, Cofton Hackett, in April 1936. The target was to finish the factory within six months at a cost of £300,000, then to employ 10,000 men to work in it. Building work commenced in August. Most of the new site, on the other side of the landing ground to the old Austin works, was covered by the main production block, which measured 1,530 by 410 feet and covered twenty acres.

Here, components were collected and assembled into Bristol Mercury VIII engines. While some components were made in other shadow factories, Austin made crankshafts, reduction gears and oil supply and control gears for the variable pitch airscrews. The first set of Austin-made components were accepted on 15 September 1937, the first complete engine tested (in Austin's own specially-designed test-beds) on 25 October, and the first engine delivered early in 1938.

Sir Herbert Austin (from 1936 Lord Austin of Longbridge) was pernickety in negotiations with the Government. The historian Roy Church has said, 'Ministers and civil servants regarded his style of negotiation to be distinctly unorthodox and difficult to handle'. Swinton thought Austin's demands outrageous - but then, the aircraft and engines were desperately needed. Chamberlain objected so much to the way in which car industry magnates negotiated shadow contracts that he refused to attend a meeting of contractors, describing it as a 'poker party'.

Austin's first shadow aircraft order was placed in May/June 1936, for 400 Fairey Battle day bombers, with parts for a further 100. Production began in October 1937 and the first aircraft was completed and test-flown on 22 July 1938, a fortnight ahead of schedule. An order for a further 363 Battles followed. From 1937 until May 1940 Lord Austin chaired the Shadow Aero Engines Committee. When Sir Ernest Lemon reviewed shadow production progress in September 1938, he found Austin behind schedule. This may have been because of a strike by 6,000 skilled workers to secure wage rates similar to those at other shadow plants. When a further Battle contract was placed with Austin on 27 June 1939, it was on condition that the labour force was increased by 5% a month.

Meanwhile in April 1936, the Government confidentially approached Rover regarding the opening of a shadow factory to make parts for the Bristol Hercules engine. This became public knowledge in July and the building of a factory at Acocks Green began in October. Production at this, 'Rover Shadow Factory No.1', began the following July. Rover did not provide any risk capital - the Government built the factory, equipped it and even recruited the workers. Rover simply had to manage and organise it. To begin with, the rate of production was deliberately kept low.

By 1938 about two million people were employed in shadow aircraft production - indeed many car firms now depended on it. But one car manufacturer was noticeably absent from the scheme. Lord Nuffield (William Morris), who had acquired Wolseley in 1927 wanted a major say in industrial rearmament policy - perhaps too big a say. The explanation of the exclusion of Nuffield really goes back to 25 July 1935, when he asked to see Cunliffe-Lister before his elevation to the peerage to discuss future prospects for Wolseley aircraft engines. The Minister replied that it was impossible to see Nuffield on the day mentioned, but gave no alternative. Nuffield felt snubbed. They eventually met in November 1935 but Swinton recorded that Nuffield was in a 'very bad mood'. So even before the shadow scheme was announced, relations between the two men were poor.

Wolseley was represented by Leonard Lord in the initial shadow discussions, but when Nuffield returned from overseas he said he favoured factories making complete engines rather than components, as the Government planned. He offered to make 2,000 Bristol engines, but this was rejected - largely because Bristol's were most unlikely to co-operate with anybody making complete power plants.

Nuffield's injury was compounded by the fact that Wolseley had been making aero engines for years. By December 1935 Wolseley were producing three types in Birmingham: the 170 hp Aquarius, the 225 hp Aries and the 250 hp Scorpio. Development work was in progress on the Scorpio II (250 hp at 10,000 feet), Leo (280 hp at 6,000 feet) and Gemini (565 hp at 9,000 feet). Wolseley engines ranged from seven to eleven cylinders, were all supercharged and all, except the smallest, had airscrew reduction gearing. The best known Wolseley engines were the Leo and Scorpio, but sales of these were disappointing - from Nuffield's point of view, because of constantly changing Air Ministry requirements. But it was commonly thought that Wolseley engines were too low powered to be of much military use, except for training aircraft.

If anything, Nuffield's existing aviation interests were an obstacle to inclusion in the shadow scheme, as he represented competition to firms like Bristol. Austin did not present such a threat.

Nuffield was also hostile to financial restrictions laid down by the Government, which he feared could bankrupt his empire. At a press conference to explain his exclusion from the shadow scheme, Nuffield explained that the Wolseley Aero Motor Factory was established in 1929 because he foresaw that it would be needed in time of national emergency. The amount of personal cash Nuffield put into marketing aircraft engines had been variously reported as 'more than £100,000', '£200,000' and '£500,000'. Whatever the truth, he certainly injected capital into this activity, founded Wolseley Aero Engines in 1935 and kept this work separate from his other enterprises, in which there were public shares.

On 14 October 1936, Wolseley announced that they were ceasing production of aero engines. This was particularly bad news for Airspeed, whose 'Envoy' twin-engined airliner performed well on Wolseley Aries nine-cylinder static radial engines and who had an order for

Below: Leonard P Lord showing the King and Queen over the Battle line at Longbridge, March 1939. With back to camera is Prime Minister Neville Chamberlain; talking with him is E L Payton, then Deputy Chairman of Austin. Lord Austin is directly between Chamberlain and the Queen. The aircraft behind the party is L5057. (BL Cars)

Werkflugplatz

7448

550 Scorpio-engined 'Envoy trainers' (to become the Oxford) pending. N S Norway visited Nuffield to try to persuade him to reverse the decision.

In his autobiography *Slide Rule*, he recalled the meeting. 'Nuffield was still furious with the Air Ministry. He grew red in the face at the thought of them and thumped the desk before him'. Norway says that Airspeed asked to take over production of Wolseley engines, but the financing of the transfer was far beyond the company's means.

Nuffield was shrewd but obstinate. He wanted to apply car production techniques to aircraft, with vast batches of absolutely identical items. He either did things 'his way' or not at all. According to his biographers Andrews and Brunner, Nuffield was 'extremely sensitive on the question of taking personal remuneration for what he regarded as national service', but he appeared to put patriotism after pride. Swinton might have been a little more diplomatic in his handling of Nuffield, but in the long run securing the car manufacturer's co-operation would have meant completely changing Government policy on shadow production and alienating all other parties.

Leonard Lord, incidentally, was taken on by Austin to manage their shadow production.

Swinton resigned in May 1938. His successor as Air Minister, Sir Kingsley Wood, announced within days of taking office that Nuffield had been persuaded to open a massive factory be-

Above: The locations and roles of the pre-war shadow factories were well known to the Germans - in fact, General Milch was shown around some of them. This view of Cofton Hackett is from a Luftwaffe target book and was probably taken from a commercial aircraft. Foreground, marked 7448, is the Battle production works. The main building measured 1,530 feet by 410 feet and covered 20 acres of the 23 acre site. Grovesley Lane runs between the plant and the shed where aircraft were stored before testing. Beyond the shed is the landing ground ('werkflugplatz') (RAF Museum)

tween Fort Dunlop and Castle Bromwich aerodrome to make Spitfires. The original intention was also to make Wellington bombers there, but none was in fact built there. Swinton claimed later that he had arranged for Vickers to run the Castle Bromwich factory and that Wood had reversed his decision. This, he claimed, cost at least 1,000 Spitfires in lost production.

The Castle Bromwich shadow factory was to be the largest of its kind in Britain, covering in all 345 acres and employing 12,000. The Nuffield Corporation bought the site from Birmingham Corporation and the first sod was dug by Wood on 14 July 1938. Nuffield put Oliver Boden, Morris Motors' Vice-Chairman, in charge. An initial order for 1,000 Spitfires was placed on 12 April 1939.

War Again

Birmingham's aircraft industry was getting into its stride when war came. Rover's factory in Acocks Green had been working for two years and the builders were at their second plant, in Solihull, and at the massive Nuffield factory in Castle Bromwich. At Longbridge, Battle production was well advanced and deep air raid shelter tunnels to accommodate 15,000 workers were being dug.

AUSTIN

The scale of wartime production for aeronautical purposes was colossal. At least 2,700 aircraft were built, plus thousands of engines, sub-assemblies and components for other aircraft.

From February 1940 the Fairey Battles were flown from the aerodrome at Cofton Hackett to RAF Worcester for testing. This decision was probably made because Cofton Hackett was very small, with a maximum run of only 1,200 feet. The railway cutting on the eastern side produced hazardous downdraughts. It was failure to counter this downdraught while approaching to land in 1939 that caused Austin's chief test pilot, Capt Neville Stack AFC, to crash into the side of this cutting in a Battle, suffering compound fractures of both legs and serious facial injuries. This incident may have been in L5254, which is known to have crashed before delivery.

The Battle was found to be hopelessly under-powered and outclassed when in action during the German advance through France in 1940, and on 7 November the Battle contract was cut by 334 aircraft. A final order for 100 aircraft was processed before the line closed in December. Austins claimed after the war that they had built 1,229 Battles at Longbridge between September 1938 and December 1940. We have been able to identify 1,029, which are listed in an Appendix.

After the completion of the Battles, 300 Hawker Hurricane Mk.IIB fighters (and the equivalent of another 200 in components and wing assemblies) were made. The first was flown from Cofton Hackett to Elmdon by Stack's successor, Geoffrey Alington, on 8 October 1940. The Hurricanes are believed to have been the last aircraft to be flown from the factory airfield.

Between December 1940 and February 1943,

191 Short Stirling Mk.I bombers were made, followed between December 1942 and October 1944 by 429 Mk.II aircraft. Final assembly of these aircraft, and the Lancasters that followed them, was carried out in a factory at Marston Green, on the north side of the Birmingham-Coventry railway line. A bridge was built over the railway and the aircraft towed down a concrete track to Elmdon and flown from there. Plans to build a second hangar at Elmdon had been in hand when the airport was officially opened in July 1939; this, and another (to become known as No2 and No3 hangars) were now hurriedly erected to house the bombers. Three weighbridges, located at three corners of a triangle, used to determine the Centre of Gravity of the bombers, are still in No2 hangar.

The bridge over the railway was demolished when the line was electrified, but the remains at either side of the track may still be seen. The route from the factory to Elmdon ran under what is now the domestic movements apron of the new terminal.

Austin made 330 of that other Bomber Command mainstay, the Avro Lancaster. Lancaster production reached its peak in June 1945, when thirty-five Mk.VIIIs were delivered. An order for a further 150 Lancasters (and possibly another for 150 Lincolns) was cancelled after the Japanese capitulation.

Below: Luftwaffe photograph of the factory at Elmdon where Austin assembled bombers. The track down which they were towed to the aerodrome marked B, is clearly marked.

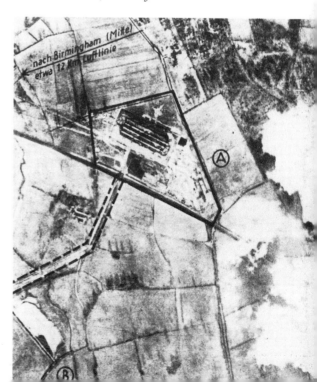

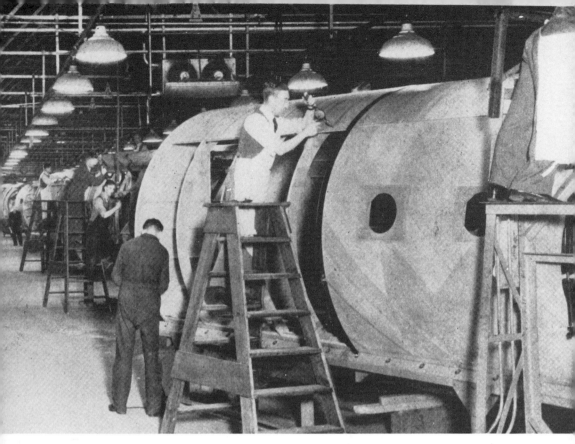

Above: Horsa glider fuselages being constructed at Longbridge.
Below: Lancaster assembly at Longbridge.

Top: The end of the Stirling wing assembly line at Long-bridge, with fuselage production in the background.

Right: A newly completed Stirling at Elmdon.

Below: the last Austin-built Stirling and the workers who assembled it, at Elmdon.

Austin also made 1,100 Miles Master wing and centre sections, 3,000 Bristol Beaufighter wing and centre sections (this task alone involving 1,060 workers), and the fuselages for 365 Horsa gliders. These fuselages were made in the West Works (now the Body Plant).

At maximum production, the Austin Aero Engine factory's 2,000 employees at Longbridge made 100 engines and 275 sets of sub-assemblies a week. In all, 14,300 Mercury and Pegasus engines were made, incorporating more than seven million Longbridge-made parts, plus 42,185 engine sets. Longbridge also turned out balloon cable cutters, landing gears, components for Rolls-Royce engines and gears for Rotol propellers, gun turrets, 15,000 fuel and oil tanks and 122,000 exhaust rings for Bristol engines.

Vital assembly processes were carried out in tunnels sixty feet underground, safe from bombing.

On 13 November 1940 the factory received its only air attack, when six employees were killed and twenty-five injured in a daylight raid. Some dispersal of production had already taken place before this raid and ten other sites (not counting Elmdon) were used, although almost three-quarters of the workforce remained at Longbridge.

At the end of the war, a York transport aircraft was converted by Austin and Avro to investigate the type's suitability for delivering cars to overseas customers. Three Austin Tens, weighing under three tons, could be carried.

But Mr Dalton's budget in the autumn of 1945 led Austin to announce that the outlook for car sales was so bleak that the firm would forego its three-month option to buy the Cofton Hackett shadow factory, in case somebody else could use it to create jobs.

ROVER

The first Hercules engine components were machined in January 1940. By September the Solihull buildings were virtually complete, and in the following month the first completely Rover-made Hercules was tested.

Rover was closely involved in the development of the gas turbine jet. Its share of the work moved to Lancashire in early 1941, though, to minimise the risk of bombing. Nevertheless, six development W.2B engines were built at Tyseley before the move.

Incidentally, the first meeting of the secret Gas Turbine Collaboration Committee, the body aimed at co-ordinating the work of all the firms involved, was held at the Midland Hotel in New Street, on 1 November 1941.

By the close of 1944 Rover had agreed with the Government that it would have first refusal on the Solihull site when it was released from war use, and that it would be the post-war centre of the company's operations.

CASTLE BROMWICH

Progress towards beginning Spitfire production at Castle Bromwich was slow and troubled. The original production target was sixty Spitfires a week, but this was cut to thirty when it was decided that bombers would also be built there - a decision which itself delayed aircraft production as building designs had to be rescaled to take the size of large bombers into account.

Drawings were late and inappropriate to the scale of production envisaged. Many modifications were arrived at by trial and error. The continuous uprating of the Rolls-Royce Merlin which powered the Spitfire made frequent airframe modifications necessary, entailing costly and time-consuming modifications to jigs, tools and fixtures. In March 1940 Oliver Boden was succeeded as manager of the factory by his assistant, Herbert Clark.

There was friction between Nuffield personnel and staff at Supermarine's factory at Southampton, particularly as demands for parts to keep the Southampton line going disrupted progress at Castle Bromwich and delayed completion of the first Birmingham-made Spitfire.

Relations between Castle Bromwich and the Ministry of Aircraft Production were strained, as well. MAP officials thought the hierarchy at Castle Bromwich was unhelpful.

On 11 May 1940 Churchill appointed Lord Beaverbrook Minister of Aircraft Production. Back in 1929 Beaverbrook had launched an Empire Crusade to promote the cause of Imperial unity, his strongest political belief. Early on he recruited Sir William Morris (later Lord Nuffield). Beaverbook suggested that the two men should run the campaign together, but Morris never took up the offer. Now the two strong-willed, blunt men were dealing with each other again.

The then Vice-Chairman of Morris Motors, Miles Thomas (later Lord Thomas of Remenham) has told the historian Alfred Price of how matters came to a head on 17 May: 'Beaverbrook rang Nuffield and demanded to know why no Spitfires had yet emerged from the Castle Bromwich factory. By chance I happened to be in Nuffield's office at Cowley when the call came, and he passed me the extension earpiece so that I could hear what was being said. Nuffield opened up with a vociferous defence of the Castle Bromwich operation and said, in effect, that Beaverbrook could have either the

Spitfires or the modifications, but not both. Then with a touch of sarcasm, as though he was playing his ace of trumps, Nuffield ended 'Perhaps you would like me to give up control of the Spitfire factory?' And Beaverbrook with his Canadian drawl jumped straight in and replied 'Nuffield, that's very generous of you. I accept!'. There was a click in the earpiece and the line went dead'.

Price's narrative continues, 'Nuffield went white as a sheet. He had been out-manoeuvred, and he knew it'. Control of Castle Bromwich was handed to Vickers.

This account conflicts with that given by A J P Taylor in his biography of Beaverbrook. According to Taylor, some time after the Ministry of Aircraft Production was formed, its branch at Harrogate reported that production at Castle Bromwich, under Nuffield, was unsatisfactory. The Ministry in London replied that Castle Bromwich had been taken out of Nuffield's hands three weeks before and its equipment removed elsewhere. No written order or record had been made. The transfer provoked Nuffield to storm into Stornoway House (Beaverbrook's offices, used by the MAP in 1940) and threaten to have Beaverbrook sacked. Beaverbrook replied there was nothing he would like better. Nuffield appealed to Churchill, with mention of the sums he contributed to Conservative Party funds, to be told by the Prime Minister 'I cannot interfere with the manufacture of aircraft'.

The ten Spitfires planned to be made at Castle Bromwich in June 1940 were completed, the first reaching the RAF on the 27th. Twenty-three aircraft followed in July, with thirty-seven in August and fifty-six in September. A further 500 Spitfires were ordered on 22 June 1940.

In the early hours of 9 August, Birmingham received the first of seventy-seven raids it was to suffer until April 1943. A lone bomber, probably looking for the Spitfire factory, ditched its load on Erdington. On the 13th the Luftwaffe 'pathfinder' unit Kampfgruppe 100 became operational at Vannes in Brittany after a move from Lüneberg. Its first mission was to seek out Fort Dunlop and Castle Bromwich, using twenty-one Heinkel He 111s. The Spitfire factory was bombed at about 2330. Nineteen 50kg bombs fell, damaging 'F' and 'Q' blocks and machinery in 'D' block. Although the all-clear was sounded at 0002, bombing was still going on - we know from German sources that the flights of bombers were spaced at half-hourly intervals. Eight workers were killed, forty-one seriously injured and 100 less so. This raid prompted the decision to disperse production.

The sites used included a carpet factory in Kidderminster, the old prison at Worcester, silk stocking and celluloid doll factories in Leicestershire, the Midland Red bus depot at Shrewsbury (which had to be vacated when the Severn flooded!), Dudley Zoo and an old iron foundry at Wellington.

The Spitfire factory was visited again by KG100 on 24/25 August. Twelve He 111s took off between 2300 and 0100. Cloud prevented the crews from seeing their objective but nevertheless they dropped eighteen High Explosive bombs. Ten He 111s of KG100 returned on 26/27; this time 'large fires and a high jet of flame' were seen. KG100 returned to Birmingham on many subsequent occasions, but rarely had specific targets within the city.

A further 800 Spitfires, some for use in the tropics and some for photo reconnaissance work, were ordered on 24 October 1940. Despite the initial problems, production gradually mounted; the 500th Spitfire made in Castle Bromwich left the line in February 1941 and the 1,000th in July. By the end of 1941 some 1,298 had been finished.

Among the many famous visitors to Castle Bromwich during the war were the American President's wife, Mrs Eleanor Roosevelt, and Winston Churchill, who came on Friday 26 September 1941. Churchill's secretary, Sir John Colville, recorded a display by a Hurricane and a Spitfire in his diary: 'Their performance was so daring as to be positively frightening and we all shuddered as Henshaw, the Spitfire pilot, flew over us upside down, some 40 feet from the ground'.

This display is mentioned by Henshaw in his book *Sigh for a Merlin - Testing the Spitfire*, which is devoted to his years test-flying at Castle Bromwich.

During 1942 Castle Bromwich turned out about fifty Spitfires a week. In all, more than 11,500 Spitfires were built at Castle Bromwich and its associated shadow factories - more than half of all those built. The exact number of Birmingham-made Spitfires is not clear. Many sources say 11,939, but in almost all cases it has been ascertained that they are quoting one historian. This figure seems too high. Programmes for post-war 'At Home' displays gave 11,694 and Vivian Bird's history of Birmingham gives 11,555. Our estimate is approximately 11,569.

The last Castle Bromwich Spitfire, PK614, was test flown on 30 November 1945.

In September 1941 200 Lancaster Mk.II bombers were ordered. Alex Henshaw has claimed responsibility for the short concrete strips at Castle Bromwich that were built for these bombers, the first of which was tested on 22 October 1943. The requirement for this batch was changed to B.III in February 1943, 49

Above: Lancaster production at Castle Bromwich. The nearest aircraft is HK649.

Left: The first Castle Bromwich built Lancaster, HK535.

Below: Fuselages of Spitfire F.22s (serials visible range from PK572 to '581) at Castle Bromwich (all via Richard R Leader)

Above: Mk.IX Spitfires in the NH serial range dominate this view of the apron outside Castle Bromwich Flight Shed in the spring of 1944.
Below: Aerial view of the Flight Shed at Castle Bromwich. (both via Richard R Leader)

but they were completed as B.I aircraft between October 1943 and February 1945. There followed an order for 200 B.Is, of which ninety-nine were delivered between 21 February and 22 August 1945. The remainder of the order was cancelled. Peak Lancaster production was twenty-five in December 1944, at which time WA Dixon was the Resident Director.

Two later orders were also cancelled: the first, placed in December 1943 was for 100 B.IV/V aircraft, and the second, placed in March 1944, was for 150 Mk.IV/V. In all, 299 Lancasters were manufactured at Castle Bromwich and another twelve assembled from parts made elsewhere.

Sad to relate, sabotage was not unknown at Castle Bromwich. In June 1944 wires in a Lancaster were found to be cut. This, and two later incidents, was traced to a disgruntled workman; Alex Henshaw has told how a large split-pin found in the magneto distributor housing of a Spitfire which nearly cost him his life 'could only have been sabotage at the point of assembly'.

Surplus labour in the Flight Sheds was used to repair Wellington bombers for the Brooklands Repair Organisation. The first of seventy-one machines was flight-tested on 31 July 1943.

By June 1944 the plant had the highest output of any aircraft factory in the United Kingdom - 320 Spitfires and twenty Lancasters a month.

At the end of the war, most of the factory was sold to Fisher & Ludlow Ltd, which BMC acquired in 1953. Some of the site was bought by Dunlop, to be used for research.

WOLSELEY

It has been reported that Wellington bombers were made under licence at the Washwood Heath factory, but this has not been substantiated. Wolseley did, however, make glider wings in conjunction with LMS, LNER and the Craven Carriage Works of Sheffield. The King and Queen visited the factory on 18 April 1940. Much of Wolseley's wartime production effort was devoted to tanks.

SERCK

Serck Radiators Ltd of Warwick Road, Tyseley, made large numbers of aircraft radiators and air coolers - notably all those fitted to Hurricanes and Spitfires in the Battle of Britain. Although close to the heavily bombed BSA works, Serck production was not much disrupted by the Luftwaffe.

SU CARBURETTORS

SU Carburettors, which when war broke out employed 700, was the only producer of Spitfire and Hurricane carburettors in 1940. All Merlin engines were fitted with SU carburettors

Below: Spitfire Mk.VC ER810 at Castle Bromwich, late 1942. (via R R Leader)

Above: An impression of the size of the production halls at Castle Bromwich is given by this 1945 view, showing Spitfire LF.XVIEs approaching completion. (via R R Leader)

until 1943, when they were superceded by Bendix ones. The factory in Wood Lane was bombed in November 1940 but the works brigade contained the fire. A few days later the firm evacuated to Shirley, occupying premises requisitioned from the Co-Operative Wholesale Society. Here the workforce increased to 1,500. The firm also made carburettors for Rolls-Royce Vulture and Peregrine and Napier Sabre and Dagger engines.

LUCAS

Lucas opened an aviation department at Great King Street in July 1938 to carry out sub-contract work for Austin - primarily 450 sets of equipment for the Battle, consisting of instrument, lighting, starting and bomb panels, ammunition boxes, wireless trays and crates for accumulators and dynamos. Again at Great King Street, Lucas began preparations in September 1938 to make sub-assemblies of the Spitfire wing-section, for use at Castle Bromwich. In late 1939 Great King Street started making Boulton & Paul hydraulically operated gun turrets. This work was later transferred to south Wales. Orders for 4,242 gun turrets and 3,982 cupolas for use on Defiants, Hudsons, Halifaxes and Albemarles were received in February 1940, to be executed at Formans Road, Sparkhill.

On 14 May 1940 top secret instructions were received from the Rover company, acting on the authority of the Ministry of Aircraft Production. This was the beginning of Lucas's contribution to the development of the jet propulsion gas turbine. Broadly speaking, Lucas's role was to develop the combustion and fuel system. The purpose of the work was kept so secret that a deputation of workers asked the management to assure them that it was to help the war effort. Even at a late stage at least one Lucas official of high rank still suspected he was working on a submarine engine! Because of the risk from bombing, the Lucas share of the work at Shaftmoor Lane, Birmingham, was transferred to Lancashire in 1942.

Pending the start-up of Spitfire production at Castle Bromwich, the Lucas sub-assemblies were sent to Supermarines at Eastleigh. The machine shops at Castle Bromwich were managed by Lucas after the factory was taken away from Nuffield. During the autumn of 1940, because of the risk from bombing, Lucas's Spitfire sub-assembly work moved to part of Cadbury's factory at Bournville.

By the end of the war 12,500 wing sub-assemblies for Spitfires had been made by Lucas. Each sub-assembly had 500 components. Dramatically improved production techniques enabled Lucas to cut the price from £4,433 to £220 by April 1943.

A Spitfire named *King of the Air* was paid for by Lucas employees in Birmingham.

GLIDERS

The Birmingham Carriage Co, the Co-Operative Wholesale Society and A C Motors Ltd jointly built fourteen General Aviation G.A.L.49 Hamilcar gliders.

RAF Activity in the Second World War

CASTLE BROMWICH

The resident fighter squadron, 605, moved to its war station on 27 August 1939. When war was declared, No 14 Elementary and Reserve Flying Training School combined with Nos 20 and 44, became No 14 Elementary Flying Training School and moved to Elmdon on 10 September. The move was made because the proximity of the balloon barrage prevented solo flying by pupils at Castle Bromwich.

Blenheims of 90 Squadron, Upwood, were temporarily based at Castle Bromwich on 26 September.

After Castle Bromwich was transferred to 70 Group, Army Co-Operation Command, No 7 Anti-Aircraft Co-Operation Unit arrived on 30 April 1940. Its personnel had assembled at Ringway and it used a collection of aircraft that had shortly before been impressed into military service. While the Unit's headquarters and maintenance bases were here, many of its aircraft were dispersed across the country, helping with the training of gun crews and calibration of

guns, searchlights and radar. The civil types were gradually replaced or supplemented by Masters, Battles and Lysanders.

In March 1943 No 7 AACU was joined by No 6 AACU, with Oxfords and Magisters. From 1 June the station was administered by Fighter Command. The AACUs, plus No 8 AACU, were amalgamated into 577 Squadron on 1 December 1943. Detachments were based at Wrexham, Sealand, Montford Bridge, Shobdon, Bodorgan and Ipswich. The squadron received Hurricanes, Spitfires, Vengeances and Beaufighters and was finally disbanded on 15 June 1946.

No 116 Squadron perhaps also maintained a detachment here in 1941. It has been reported that 567 Squadron, another anti-aircraft co-operation squadron, maintained a detachment at Castle Bromwich in 1943-44 with Vengeance, Battle, Oxford, Hurricane and Martinet aircraft. Another, 285 Squadron, kept Oxfords, Martinets, Defiants and Hurricanes at Castle Bromwich from January to November 1944 and from January 1945 until disbandment on 26 June 1945. 3507 Servicing Unit was another wartime resident.

ELMDON

The first wartime arrivals were Wellingtons of 99 Squadron, dispersed from Mildenhall, on 9 September 1939. No 14 EFTS moved in from Castle Bromwich the next day. On 15 September the Wellingtons moved on to Newmarket and on the 16th civil flying formally stopped.

The mainstay of No 14 EFTS throughout the war was the Tiger Moth - and plenty of them, as can be seen in the relevant Appendix. As many of the aircraft served with several units during their lifetimes, we think many Tigers were at Elmdon for months, rather than years. The School operated a Relief Landing Ground at Hockley Heath (q.v.). We suspect that this was in connection with the construction at Elmdon of two hard runways, 4,260 and 4,170 feet long, principally for the use of Stirling and Lancaster bombers test-flown from there. The School disbanded on 1 February 1946.

Left: This snapshot of a naval trainee at Elmdon is particularly interesting because the terminal building has camouflage netting draped over it. The Tiger Moth is N6449 'N'. (Lt Cdr L J Kelly)

Opposite, above: Try not to look at the camera! The only identifiable Tiger Moth in this Elmdon view is N6546 'F'. Probably taken before May 1940, this view shows no sign of construction work on numbers 2 and 3 hangars. (Lt Cdr L J Kelly)

Below: Pilots running towards their Tiger Moths at Elmdon, in 1939 or 1940. The only Tiger that is identifiable is N5454. However, this picture is made particularly interesting by the three Dragon Rapides parked to the edge of the tarmac. Left to right, they are G-AEXO (impressed from North Eastern Airways Ltd for 24 Squadron, Hendon, March 1940); G-AERZ of Air Commerce Ltd, Heston, and G-AFEO (impressed as X8506 from North Eastern Airways Ltd, March 1940). (Lt Cdr L J Kelly)

HOCKLEY HEATH

This Relief Landing Ground, ten miles south-south-east of Birmingham, on the A34 Birmingham to Stratford road, opened in 1941. It consisted of one Nissen and five Laing huts and six blister hangars. It offered runs of 4,000 feet. From August 1942 it was used as a Relief Landing Ground by No 2 Central Flying School, whose main base was at Church Lawford, near Dunchurch. The School used Oxfords and Tutors. After No 14 EFTS's spell of residence, from 29 October 1942 to 20 December 1943, Hockley Heath was used by No 5 Glider Training School. Master IIs and Hotspur gliders were here from February 1943 or July 1944 until November 1945. Harvards of No 20 Flying Training School used the site as a Relief Landing Ground in mid-1945.

Two aircraft are known to have met their ends at Hockley Heath: Hawker Audax K7322 crashed in a forced landing on 19 November and Avro Tutor K3461 undershot landing on 11 October 1942.

One rare aircraft here during the war was the Dutch-built De Schelde Scheldemusch, which arrived in 1944. Although it sported RAF roundels and training colours, it still bore the Dutch civil registration PH-AMG. From 15 September 1945 to about May 1946 it was owned by J H V Wood, who bought it from the widow of Sqn Ldr Longbottom for £145. The Scheldemusch was delivered to Chadwick End, Knowle, base of glider repairer Don Burgoyne.

Early one morning it was towed the six miles to Hockley Heath. 'It was a bit too wide and I had to weave it in and out past the lamp posts', recalled Mr Wood recently.

Between October 1945 and August 1946 it made more than a dozen local flights from Hockley Heath of up to an hour's duration, at heights ranging from 250 to 1,500 feet.

Wood stored the aircraft in a hangar he had built earlier for a Pou du Ciel, behind his father's motor business on the Stratford Road, Shirley. It was seen here in April 1947. Wood gave the Scheldemusch to his friend Flt Lt David Langford, who collected it from Wood's home at Roville, Blossomfield, Solihull. The reason for the gift is that some children broke in to Wood's shed and started to tear fabric off the aircraft and it was felt that the Scheldemusch would be safer in Langford's care. The youngsters appeared before Solihull magistrates, while the aircraft went to Lincolnshire were it is believed to have been damaged when it turned over while being taxied without the tail attached to the airframe.

Hockley Heath was abandoned as an aerodrome in 1948, but the airspace above it has often been used by local pilots for engine failure practice.

Below: Group of pilots, Elmdon. On the far right is the late Cdr A V Doneghy, who was at 14 EFTS from December 1940 to March 1941, when he proceeded to No 1 FTS, Netheravon. Identification and news of others in this group would be welcomed. (Mrs Peggy I Doneghy)

Above: The Scheldemusch, probably at Hockley Heath in about 1945. From left to right, Joe Woods, Sqn Ldr David Langford, Tony Hofton. (Science Museum, London)

WOE TO THE UNWARY ...

Pilots were warned to avoid Birmingham carefully because of the anti-aircraft balloons which were supposed to protect the city from bombing. Nevertheless, many aircraft strayed into the area and crashed, though not all of them because of the balloons.

Known incidents are, listed chronologically:

5.2.40 Blackburn Shark K5651 was abandoned and crashed six miles west of Coventry.

28.10.40 Blenheim R3840 of No 3 Ferry Pilots Pool hit a balloon cable near Birmingham.

9.11.40 Anson N9945 of the Blind Approach and Development Unit hit a balloon cable (site 3) at Stechford, after wandering off course, at 0100. Five crew killed.

30.11.40 Wellington T2893 hit trees in a forced landing after its engines failed at night near Elmdon.

12.12.40 Audax K7445 of No 9 FTS, from Hullavington, crashed after hitting a balloon cable (site 61) at Longbridge at 1630. Burnt out on impact. The trainee pilot, LAC S R Phillips (killed) had strayed twenty miles off course.

12.2.41 Hampden AD734 'K' of 83 Squadron, Scampton, abandoned after hitting a balloon cable (site 14) at 0200 after operations, 'near Birmingham'. All four crew baled out successfully, two near Elmdon and two near Longbridge.

21.3.41 Blenheim T1892 of 105 Squadron, Swanton Morley, hit a balloon cable (site 61 of 915 Squadron) just after midnight and crashed at Rednal. Aircraft was returning from operations; navigation error due to strong winds.

7.7.41 Whitley Z6476 of No 10 Operational Training Unit hit a balloon cable at Quinton at 0155 and crashed, killing six, while on a cross-country flight.

7.8.42 Wellington R1075 of No 16 Operational Training Unit wandered off track and hit a balloon cable at Erdington.

16.3.44 Halifax LW413 'KW:Q' of 425 Squadron was abandoned at Brierley Hill after an operational mission; crashed on houses at rear of 4 Adelaide Street. One civilian killed.

22.3.44 Wellington HD987 crashed on the Midland Red garage at Mill Lane, Digbeth, apparently after engine failure.

4.8.44 Master W9027 stalled at low altitude and crashed at the Parkinson-Cowan stove works, very near the pilot's home.

12.6.45 Spitfire P8916 of the Ministry of Aircraft Production, according to its official record card, took off at Castle Bromwich whilst undergoing ground trials.

Post-War Castle Bromwich

As already mentioned, 577 Squadron was at Castle Bromwich until it disbanded in June 1946. The airfield became part of RAF Reserve Command, later Home Command.

On 1 November 1947 No5 Reserve Flying School was formed here. It was operated by Birkett Air Services and flew Tiger Moths, Prentices, Ansons and (from July 1951) Chipmunks. It was disbanded on 30 June 1954.

The same types were used from 1947 by the Birmingham University Air Squadron, which was first formed as a non-flying unit in 1941. Indeed, many aircraft were exchanged by the units. The BUAS flew its Chipmunks to Shawbury on 11 March 1958 and officially moved there on the 24th.

No48 Gliding School moved in from Fosse Way in September 1945. It trained Air Training Corps cadets to fly gliders. The School became defunct on 19 September 1955.

1955 AOP Flight of 663 Squadron, which used Auster A.O.P.6 and T.7 and Chipmunk aircraft, was at Castle Bromwich from 1955 until it disbanded on 10 March 1957.

Other post-war occupants were No7 District RAF Police, the Birmingham and Warwickshire Wing of the Air Training Corps, No3605 (County of Warwick) Fighter Control Unit and No44 Reserve Centre. The ATC remained after other units left in 1958.

In post-war years Hurricane 5500M was displayed at the aerodrome gate, later to be replaced by the Castle Bromwich-made Spitfire 6457M/ML427, which is now at the Birmingham Museum of Science and Technology.

The only known post-war incident involving a visiting aircraft was on 14 January 1949, when the undercarriage of Oxford V3190 retracted after landing.

'At Home' Displays were held each year to mark the anniversary of the Battle of Britain. For example:

15 September 1945: the programme promised flying by a Spitfire Mk.XVI, height-guessing competitions involving an Oxford, drogue towing by a Vengeance Mk.IV and circuits by a Cadet glider.

16 September 1950: static, Spitfire F.Mk.22 PK623, Lincoln RF423, Harvard T.2 PT332, Seafire SX351, Wellington PG357, Prentice VS286, Hastings TG575, Dakota KN657, Anson PH533. Flying: Dakota KN371, Auster TW453, Sedbergh glider WB975, Cierva C.30A G-AHTZ from Elmdon, Honiley-based Chipmunks WB570 and WB571, 605 Squadron's Meteor WA598 and four Vampires, Spitfire 21 LA232, Lincoln RE346 and Tudor 7 VX199.

18 September 1954: the display included Austers TW453, TW528, TW530 and WE554, Meteors WA657 and WM180, Varsity WF369, Valetta VW838, Mosquito HJ971, Brigand RH767, Provost WV489, Lincolns RA684 and RE346,

Below: Demonstration by Sikorsky Hoverfly helicopter at Castle Bromwich, late 1940s. (Len Bracey)

Harvard FT156, Vampire XD516, Ansons WD419 and VP523, Oxford LX118, Prentice VS270, Balliol WN510, Tempest SN127, Hunter WT591, Canberras WH702, WJ646, WJ717, WJ724 and WV646, Firefly WB493, Sedbergh WB975, Neptune WX547, Shackletons WB818, WB824 and WB861, Valiant WP203, Hastings TG503 and VD482, Bristol Freighter VR380, Vampire VZ195, WA358 and XD627, Sunderland DP200, Cadet VM689, Sea Prince WJ348, Dragon Rapides G-AIUL, 'KOV and 'LUK, Autocrat G-AGTX, Balliol G-ANSF and a fly-past by nine Sabres.

17 September 1955: attended by 145,000. According to the programme the display featured: static, Spitfire, Chipmunk, Valetta, Harvard, Neptune, Varsity, Vampire, Provost, Mosquito, Anson, Meteor, USAF SA-16. Flying: individual Hunter, Valiant, Javelin, Beverley, Sunderland, Spitfire; formations of Canberras, Shackletons, Neptunes, Fairey Fireflys, B-29s, F-86D Sabres, F-84F Thunderjets and B-47s. The Vulcan was to have appeared but was withdrawn because of its test programme. It was an extremely windy day and a fly-past of 20 to 25 Tiger Moths could have met with disaster - two machines actually touched in flight, but fortunately for the occupants and those around them, the aircraft did not lose their place in the box formation.

14 September 1957: static were a Provost, Meteors WE927 and WL906, USAF C-119 18250, Chipmunk, Vampires WZ460 and WZ475, Hastings TG528, Mosquito TA642, Auster XK391, Balliol WN351. Flying: Hunter WP104, Comets XK663 and XK670, Valiant WZ374, Beverley XL148, Canberras WJ719, WJ723, WJ732, Victor XA919, Shackleton,

Vulcan XA904, Vampires WL496, WR217, WR272, WX204 and XK635, Meteors, F-84F Thunderjets, Sea Hawk XE449, Provosts WV674 and WV683, Viscount G-AMAV, Valetta WD171 and Chipmunks.

Her Majesty Queen Elizabeth approved a badge for RAF Castle Bromwich in March 1955. It included a sprig of broom, which once grew in profusion on the site - hence the word 'brom-wich'; a mural crown taken from the city's crest and the motto 'Supra Urbem Alae Nostrae Volant' - 'Our Wings Rise Over the City'. Her Majesty flew in on 3 August 1957 in a Queen's Flight Heron on her way to the World Scout Jamboree at Sutton Park.

In post-war years the British Industries Fair again attracted civil aircraft to Castle Bromwich. On 2 May 1949 Patrick Aviation opened a service to London (Croydon and Hendon) in conjunction with the BIF. It was operated in collaboration with Air Enterprises and International Airways.

On 9 May 1950, Westland Aircraft Ltd, in co-operation with Rotor Stations Ltd, operated what was claimed to be the first scheduled helicopter service in Britain, from the Harrods sports ground in Barnes, London, to Castle Bromwich. This service, which ceased on 19 May, was in connection with the BIF. Two services were flown on weekdays, using the Westland-Sikorsky S-51 G-ALIK commanded by Capt Kenneth Reed. Flying time was seventy-five minutes.

Three BEA Dakotas, G-AHCZ, 'IWD and 'JIC, chartered by the Cincinnati engineering company to bring agents to its Tyburn Road factory for a conference, flew in on 6 June 1957.

The last official scheduled departure was by a Chipmunk piloted by the station commander, Sqn Ldr Harry Coldbeck, on 14 March 1958. A lone glider remained in one of the hangars for a while. The station was closed on 31 March and the 350-acre site was sold to Birmingham Corporation on 21 September 1960 to be used for one of its biggest housing developments, the Castle Vale Estate. The BIF site, which then covered sixty acres, was also cleared (in 1957) and the halls flattened to make way for the new housing.

Castle Bromwich's links with its aeronautical past are not completely eradicated, though. Most of the streets and block of flats on the estate have names with aviation connotations. Alex Henshaw, the former Castle Bromwich Spitfire test pilot, unveiled a memorial to the aerodrome on 8 October 1965. The plinth incorporates the RAF badge that used to be at the entrance to the Officers' Mess. A Spitfire, Hurricane and Lightning flew over the ceremony.

This page:

Above: Tiger Moth DE840 clearly showing the 'RCY' code of 5 RFS. (Len Bracey)

Left: Parachute training from balloons (but not at this height!) often took place at Castle Bromwich in post-war years. (Len Bracey)

Below: Tiger Moths DF211 and DE840. (Len Bracey)

Opposite page:

Top: An outing for Chipmunks WB686, WB673 and WB682 of 5 RFS. (Roy Bonser)

Centre: The Castle Bromwich emergency crew, 1950s style. (Len Bracey)

Lower: The wreckage of Chipmunk WP779 at Castle Bromwich. (Len Bracey)

Above: The Queen's Heron taxying in at Castle Bromwich, August 1957. (Len Bracey)
Below: The BEA Dakotas chartered by the Cincinnati company to fly to Castle Bromwich during 1957. (Staddon Collection)

Above: The last Auster departure from Castle Bromwich (by TW455) was marred by an altercation with a parked car - see chipped propeller blade. (Len Bracey)
Below: Castle Bromwich, August 1964. Building work on the massive new housing estate is getting under way, but the 1930s RAF hangar and the British Industries Fair buildings still stand. The former aircraft factory is at the top of the photograph. (Birmingham Post & Mail)

Elmdon:
A Fresh Start

In 1946 hangar space became available at Elmdon with the closure of 14 EFTS and the end of bomber production, and Dunlop's Test Flight moved in from Honiley. The unit's purpose was to evaluate new products and enable realistic experiments to be carried out. It brought three aircraft: Wellington III BK563, Albemarle V2046 and Buckingham I KV479. The Chief Test Pilot was W H Sutcliffe, formerly of the Midland Aero Club and Rolls-Royce. The Lancaster I PB752 came in August. The usefulness of the Unit was deemed to have ended in 1949 and its aircraft were returned to the Ministry of Supply.

As early as March 1945 there was speculation as to what role Elmdon might play in post-war aviation. Leonard Faulkner said he did not see any prospect of trans-Atlantic services from Birmingham, but hoped that routes to Paris and Amsterdam would commence soon after the war. At the 1945 AGM of the Royal Aeronautical Society's Birmingham branch, held at the Edgbaston Botanical Gardens on 1 September, the newly elected Member of Parliament Julius Silverman called for the early return of Elmdon to civil operations. Control of the aerodrome was transferred to the Ministry of Civil Aviation on 19 June 1946 and a MCA Oxford visited on 8 July, when civil flying officially resumed there. The Midland Aero Club started flying again in May 1946. On 16 August 1947 the Club held an 'At Home' attended by about twenty aircraft, including Leonides-powered Oxford LX119, Avian G-ACKE, Wicko G-AENU, Puss Moth G-ABZK and Cub G-AISX.

One of the first post-war occupants was Cecil Kay Aircraft (1945) Ltd, which made most of its money from selling aircraft. It was the Midlands distributor of the Auster range of light aeroplanes and was managed by L N S Dunkerton. From May 1946 the Proctor 5 G-AHBH was used on air taxi services. A second Proctor, G-AIAA, started service on 5 September. Other aircraft which passed through its hands were Auster J/4s G-AIJK, 'IPG and 'IPK (based February 1947 - May 1948); Taylorcraft Plus D G-AHAJ; Auster Autocrats G-AGYZ, 'HHL and 'JAB; Proctor 1 G-AHVJ; Dragon Rapide G-AGZU and Aerovan IV G-AJWL. The company is believed to have ceased trading in March 1948.

In July 1946 Mercury Air Services was established by J J H Charlebois and J G Woodhill, with two Proctors, G-AHTG and 'TH. Mercury was bought by Patrick-Duval Aviation, which was founded by Capt Duval and J A M Patrick on 8 October. Patrick Duval was associated with Patrick Motors. The assets of Mercury were acquired in December 1946 and in the following month an Airspeed Consul was used to commence operations. Patrick-Duval were Miles dealers and two Aerovans were delivered in spring 1947. They were often to be seen at weekends doing pleasure flying at Elmdon, whilst charter flights were operated to the Isle of Man, Isle of Wight and the Channel Islands. With their nine seats removed, the Aerovans frequently ferried flowers from the Isles of Scilly to the Midlands.

Registered in February 1947 by E H Ludlow and L Hargreaves, Wheels and Wings began pleasure and charter work from Elmdon in November 1946, using the Auster Autocrats

Below: Dunlop's Proctor G-AHBA with Lincoln RE253 and Buckingham KV479 at Elmdon. (via C E Read)

G-AIFZ and 'IGU. The Dragon Rapide G-AIUI was added in May 1947, but operated under the name Hargreaves Airways. In September the name 'Wheels and Wings' was dropped. The new airline's initial fleet was the Rapide and the Auster J/2 Arrow G-AJAM. The Rapide crashed on 30 June 1948, in the Isle of Man, killing five of its seven passengers and the pilot, Capt C S M Herbert. Flying was suspended and the Arrow sold.

The next Elmdon operator was the Yellow Air Taxi Co Ltd. Founded in January 1948, it initially offered the Percival Q.6 G-AHOM and the Autocrat G-AHHL for charter, training and pleasure flights. The Q.6 was replaced by the Dragon Rapide G-ACPP in June 1948. In December, the Proctor V G-AHBJ joined, followed in 1950 by a Tiger Moth. Charter work ceased in 1952 when the fleet was sold.

At around this time large numbers of RAF Harvards came to Elmdon to be overhauled by Helliwells in No 3 hangar (the most easterly one).

In the late 1940s, British European Airways effectively controlled all domestic scheduled services and independent airlines operated them only with the state airline's consent. Consequently Patrick-Duval's first service, to the Isle of Man in July 1948, was under a BEA Associa-

Top: Line-up of Dunlop Test Flight aircraft at Elmdon: from left to right, Lancaster, Buckingham, Albemarle, Wellington, Proctor, Lincoln.

Above: Dunlop Test Flight aircraft and pilots at Elmdon, 1946. From left to right, Wellington BK563, Proctor G-AHBA, Lancaster RE253 and Albemarle V2046.

Below: W H Sutcliffe, Chief Test Pilot of Dunlop's Test Flight, in front of Proctor V G-AHBA, the firm's communications aircraft. (all via C E Read)

tion Agreement. Two Rapides bought in June operated the route four times weekly during the peak season. A Rapide and an Aerovan flew a tabulating machine and spare parts from Luton to Dublin for Lep Transport on 26 November.

Towards the end of 1948 Capt Duval left unexpectedly to take a flying job in Africa, so on 21 January 1949 the airline was renamed Patrick Aviation. The two Consuls were sold in December 1948 to Air Enterprises, who the following month sold three Dragon Rapides to Patrick. J A M Patrick was now the only shareholder, with W Towler and R G Whitfield as co-directors. R A (Ron) Pickler was General Manager and H A McCarthy the Chief Engineer. Four captains (Tommy Pike, Wally Evans and Dicky Hill were three of them) and twelve staff were employed, many on Patrick's flourishing second-hand aircraft business.

In January 1947 Ernest Lees and F A Hill founded Lees-Hill Aviation and offered the Auster Autocrat G-AIJZ for charter and pleasure flights. The Aerovan G-AJWI was added in June. On 22 January 1948 Lees, with William Critchlow, registered the Birmingham Aero Club, which had in fact been active since September 1947, using two Austers previously operated by Wheels and Wings. These Austers were joined by the Lees-Hill Autocrat and two others. In April 1948 the Club was renamed the Warwickshire Aero Club and took three Austers (G-AIGU, 'IJK and 'IPK) whilst Lees-Hill retained G-AIJZ and 'JVV. For the 1948 season Lees-Hill replaced the Aerovan with the Rapides G-AGLR, 'GPI and 'HGF, and operated them to Sandown, the Isle of Man and the Channel Islands. Lees-Hill was much in evidence at Elmdon on summer weekends, offering joy flights. On Whit Monday (29 May) 1950, for example, they took up about 600 people. One of the Rapides was sold in May 1949. The Warwickshire Aero Club has continued to operate independently right up to the present day, with the Austers being superceded by a succesion of aircraft including Piper Colts and Cessna 150s.

By 1949, councils in the West Midlands were concerned that Birmingham was not included in the British European Airways route network. BEA claimed that it had so far not served the city because it had neither the money nor the equipment. Following a conference, fourteen councils sent a deputation to the Minister of Civil Aviation, Lord Pakenham (now Longford), on 24 September 1948. Shortly after, he announced that BEA would open a thrice-weekly Birmingham - Paris (Le Bourget) route on 8 April 1949.

BEA set up shop in Birmingham on 19 February, when Tommy Staddon arrived to prepare for the Paris opening. From early on, his impression was that BEA was merely responding to political pressure and was not enthusiastic about operating from Birmingham.

In anticipation of the Paris opening, customs facilities and Standard Beam Approach were installed, parts of the the main runway resurfaced, a homing beacon erected and about 200 trees on the south side of the A45 Birmingham - Coventry road felled to clear the approach. On 5 April, BEA's Chief Pilot at Manchester, Capt Geoff Greenhalgh, together with six of his captains, brought a Dakota to Elmdon on a proving flight and then flew to Paris. The route was to be shared with Air France, which also made some familiarisation flights.

On the big day, 8 April, BEA's new Chairman, Lord Douglas of Kirtleside, flew to Birmingham in the Dove G-ALFU and was met by local councillors and MPs. The service originated from Manchester, from where Capt Greenhalgh flew the Dakota G-AHCU.

While some of the guests accompanied the Press on the inaugural flight, others went for a dinner at the Council House. To pay its way, the route would need an average load of 70% - 17 or 18 passengers on each flight. Performance was to be reviewed after six months. Pakenham warned that the survival of the route depended on it being well used — 'It is up to you'.

The first Paris flight with fare-paying passengers (four from Manchester and nine who joined at Birmingham) was on 11 April. The return fare on this first international route out of the Midlands was £18, which included a cold meal in each direction. The journey took 2 hours 20 minutes. Air France's aircraft also continued on to Manchester and, like BEA's, operated three times a week - Tuesday, Thursday and Saturday.

Also on 11 April Patrick Aviation flew its first Birmingham - Jersey scheduled service, under an Associate Agreement with BEA. A Dragon Rapide with nine passengers left an hour before BEA's Paris flight. Other Patrick routes opened by agreement with BEA in 1949 were to Blackpool and Southampton, both with Rapides. The Isle of Man service was also continued, from June, again with Rapides. In town, Patrick opened a booking office in Paradise Street.

On 2 May 1949 Aer Lingus opened a weekday Dakota service from Dublin. The first flight was by EI-ACL. The return fare was £10-16s (£10.80). This was not the first visit to Elmdon by the Irish carrier, though, as on 7 April two Dakotas had brought fifty-one motor agents in to visit Standard's Vanguard production line at Coventry. Under an agreement between the British and Irish Governments routes to the Republic were operated exclusively by Aer Lingus, so BEA did not participate on the route.

Above: Midland Aero Club's Taylorcraft Plus D G-AHVR. Note that the terminal building is still in camouflage. (via John Nicholds)

Right: Dignitaries with Patrick Aviation's Consul G-AIOV before it opened the service to the Isle of Man. (Birmingham Post & Mail)

Below: Demonstration at Elmdon by St John's Ambulance volunteers, with Patrick Aviation Rapide G-AHGH. (Birmingham Post & Mail via Patrick Collection)

Above: Aer Lingus Dakota EI-AFB. (Lucas)
Below: The first international service - a BEA Dakota G-AHCU - passes over Elmdon en route for Paris. Note that the tower is still in its wartime camouflage. The Dove is G-ALFU in which BEA's new Chairman, Lord Douglas Kirtleside arrived. (Birmingham Post & Mail)

Above: Lord Pakenham addresses the crowd before the inaugural BEA flight to Paris, 8 April 1949.
Below: Departure of an Air France Dakota from Elmdon - possibly the first.

The initial commercial response to the BEA Paris service was indifferent, and the airline soon warned that it would have to be withdrawn by the autumn if bookings did not improve. By September 500 passengers had been flown in each direction. During the 1949/50 winter only two flights a week, on Mondays and Fridays, were operated. The third frequency was restored in April 1950, but the route lost £20,000 in its first year and BEA ruled out the possibility of opening further Continental services out of Birmingham. A spokesman said, 'We were subjected to great pressure by the city authorities, but the rosy picture they painted for the future had not materialised'. A BEA service to Belfast opened on 26 April 1950. Operated on weekdays with Dakotas, fare-paying passengers were taken from 1 May. Flying time was 1 hour 45 minutes and the single fare was £4-15s (£4.75). Extra Sunday flights operated from 14 May to 17 September.

The Royal Aero Club had announced on 11 April 1949 that large-scale air racing would be re-introduced. The first major meeting was to be held at Elmdon from Friday 29 July to Monday 1 August, a Bank Holiday weekend. The choice of Birmingham as the venue for the National Air Races was appropriate, as the city had been due to host the 1939 races and the Midland Aero Club was about to celebrate its fortieth birthday. The Club, now boasting 400 members and six aircraft (three two-seat Aus-

ters, an Autocrat and two Tiger Moths), was to play a major role in the local organisation of the races, under the leadership of its President, Wilf Sutcliffe.

The highlight of the meeting was the King's Cup race, for which for the first time the finalists were selected from heats or eliminating rounds, spaced throughout the season. In all seventy-seven aircraft were entered for the National Air Races, six from overseas. Of the thirty-six entries for the King's Cup itself, two were from private owners who were members of the Midland Aero Club: W G Breen-Turner with his Messenger 2A G-AILI and Arthur Harrison with his Auster 5 G-ALFA. However, neither reached the final, which J N Somers won in the Gemini G-AKDC at 164.25 mph.

The Kemsley Trophy was won by Sqn Ldr Neville Duke in the Hawker P.1040 VP401; the Royal Auxiliary Air Force Squadron Race for the Cooper Trophy was won by Flg Off W Bowden of 502 (County of Ulster) Squadron in the Spitfire F.Mk.22 PK716 at 325 mph; the Grosvenor Challenge Cup was captured by F Dunkerley with the Gemini 1A G-AKKB at 144.5 mph; the Norton Griffiths Challenge Trophy went to the Czech Jan Andrle with his Aero 45 OK-DCL; and the Air League Challenge Cup to P G Lawrence with Firebrand EK621.

Advertised as the world's fastest race, the SBAC Challenge Cup, on 1 August, open to any

Below left: Captain Geoff Greenhalgh and colleagues at Elmdon, 5 April 1949.

Below right: Short Scion G-AEZF was resident in the late 1940s. (S S Caro)

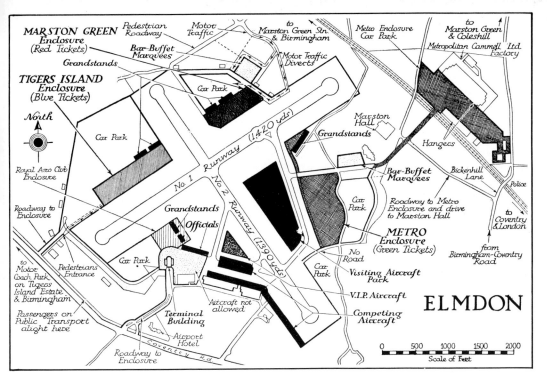

The meeting - the largest yet to be staged at
any UK airport - attracted 120,000 visitors.
Hopes that it would be repeated at Elmdon in
1950 were, however, dashed when the Royal
Aero Club announced that it would next be
held at Wolverhampton.

jet, was taken by Wade with the P.1040 VP401
at 510 mph. His rivals in this event were Derry
and Cunningham - names to conjure with.

*The above map produced to show the arrange-
ments of the air racing events is also of interest
in that it shows the state of development of
the airfield and environs in mid-1949.*

In November 1949 the Ministry of Civil
Aviation told Patrick Aviation that BEA would
operate the Jersey route from the following year.
As the route had been highly successful, this
was a disaster for Patrick. The MP for Kings
Norton, A R Blackburn, raised the issue in the
Commons. Patrick Aviation suggested that its
Rapides be used as back-up aircraft in case
demand did not justify using a Dakota, but the
Minister rejected the idea. Some Patrick Aviation
staff were laid off. Thus Patrick's only scheduled
route in the summer 1950 season was to the
Isle of Man. It decided to pull out of this
Associate Agreement, which it had shared since
May 1949 with North-West Airlines, in October
1950. Much of the fleet was sold and activities
generally run down until operations ceased in
early 1953. A final, unsuccessful attempt to
restart scheduled services was made in December 1952, when Patrick applied for licences to
operate various routes out of Birmingham, including one to Amsterdam using Dakotas and
Rapides. North-West resolved to keep its service,

although it had experienced poor loads and had
no guarantee that its own Associate Agreement
with BEA would be renewed when it expired in
March 1951. Its summer service restarted in
May 1953, now using Lancashire Aircraft Corporation Dakotas, instead of Rapides. The route
also operated in 1955, recommencing in June.

KLM's second visit, more than a decade
after the first, was when a Douglas Skymaster,
the largest aircraft yet to land at Elmdon, took
fifty-one members of the Birmingham Philhar-
monic Orchestra to Holland on 30 June 1950.
Twenty-eight other musicians travelled in a
Dakota.

Meanwhile the regular foreign operators at
Elmdon seemed to be thriving. About 4,000
passengers used the Aer Lingus Dublin service
during its first six months - 1,129 during July
alone, when ten extra flights were laid on. This
encouraging response enabled Aer Lingus to
maintain its frequency during the 1949/50
winter and operate two flights daily during
summer 1950. In October 1951 Aer Lingus
opened an all-cargo Dublin - Birmingham service.
This was the first of several unsuccessful freight
services out of Birmingham, and it survived
only until the following autumn.

From 30 June 1951 Air France operated a summer weekend service from Manchester via Elmdon to Dinard and La Baule. The Birmingham - Manchester leg was dropped from the Paris route from 20 April 1952. From 28 June that year Birmingham also enjoyed its own route to Dinard and La Baule.

BEA Dakotas operated daily flights from Manchester via Birmingham to Jersey from 13 May 1950, with extra services when needed.

Helicopter operations by BEA to a specially built 'Rotorstation' at Hay Mills, 3½ miles east of the city centre, began on 1 June 1951. The 'Rotorstation', on Haybarn Recreation Ground, covered about 7,000 square yards. Birmingham Corporation built the service road from Hob Moor Road, while BEA put up the buildings. The three-seat Sikorsky S-51 helicopters were maintained at Elmdon - the first BEA aircraft to be so. The captains, John Theilmann, Dennis Bryon, John Fay and Ron Dibb, lived in caravans parked behind the hangars at Elmdon. Seats were offered on the positioning flights between Hay Mills and Elmdon at 7s-6d (37½p) and were very popular with local people. The demonstration flight on 28 May had to depart from Elmdon because Hay Mills was not complete. The flight was diverted to Denham because of fog in the London suburbs, but continued to Northolt after a twenty minute wait. The single fare from Hay Mills to either Northolt or Heathrow was £2-10s (£2.50), compared with £1-17s-9d (£1.88) for a Birmingham - London First Class rail ticket. Services left Hay Mills at 0700, 1200 and 1615, arriving at Northolt at 0810, 1310 and 1725 and at Heathrow twenty minutes later. Northbound services left Heathrow at 1010, 1415 and 1850, calling at Northolt ten minutes later and reaching Hay Mills at 1145, 1550 and 2025.

Between June 1951 and March 1952, 802 flights were scheduled, of which 623 operated, carrying 1,082 passengers and a ton of freight. Most cancellations were caused by the weather. The last service was on 5 April 1952. From 9 April it was replaced by a freight once-daily service from Elmdon to Northolt and Heathrow. A four-seat Bristol 171 helicopter made a proving flight to Birmingham in May 1953 and was introduced on the route on 13 July. Capt Jock Cameron flew the first Bristol 171 service in G-AMWH. Calls at Northolt were put on an 'on demand' basis at this time, probably reflecting the run-down of commercial aviation there. Helicopter mail, under the Air Letter service, was flown on the route from November but the last 171 flight was on 14 January 1954.

Lees-Hill, with its two Rapides and two Austers, was taken over by the Wolverhampton-orientated Modern Transport on 5 September 1951, to create Don Everall (Aviation) Ltd. During its first full summer, in 1952, the Rapides G-AGDP and 'GLR were principally used on routes from the Midlands to the Isle of Man and the Channel Isles, and on charters. In 1953 BEA invited Don Everall to share in the operation of its London route, which it did with Rapides from 1 June.

Rare birds based at Elmdon in the post-war years included two Cierva C.30A Autogiros, G-ACUU and 'HTZ. The first was owned by G S Baker and came in April 1950. In July 1951 it was exhibited in the 'Fifty Years of Flying' show at Hendon. It left Elmdon on 20 March 1964. G-AHTZ was owned by Rota Towels Ltd and used by autogiro enthusiast H J Barnes. It was based there from July 1949 until it burnt out at Elmdon on 4 March 1958. Another rarity was S S Caro's Short Scion 2 G-AEZF which was resident from April 1948 to June 1950. Prominent owners included C G M Alington, who had test-flown Stirlings at Elmdon during the war, who owned Miles M.5 Sparrow Hawk G-ADNL, Stinson Reliant G-AFHB and D.H.90A Dragonfly G-AIYJ. Another was Thomas Carlyle, with Auster J/1N Alpha G-AGTP, Autocrat G-AGWY and Messenger 2A G-AJEY.

The dramatic increase in scheduled air services created problems in the early 1950s for the Midland Aero Club, which feared it might have to move away. It should be remembered that Air Traffic Control then was not able to handle anything like the volume of traffic that is taken for granted today. On 8 September 1951 the Club held a highly successful air display at Elmdon, attended by 30,000. Club aircraft at this time included the Tiger Moth G-AJKD, Auster G-AHVR and Plus D G-AHVS. Although there was an event to mark the Coronation in May 1953, the Club was unable to stage further big displays. Until the advent of the big flying schools at Oxford, Hamble and Perth, the Club continued to offer instruction. However, tightened security arrangements caused the gate from Elmdon Lane to Hangar Road, behind the hangars, to be locked. This meant one had to drive several miles to get from the clubhouse to the airport. This inconvenience led to a running down of flying until the Club was only a social centre.

Bus services from the city to Elmdon had begun in 1949, the fare being included in the cost of the air ticket. The original town terminus was Queen's Drive, which ran through the middle of the old New Street station. The growth of traffic warranted the building of an air terminal next to the Civic Centre in Broad Street, at a cost of £16,447. It was opened on

30 October 1951. BEA, BOAC, Air France and KLM had offices there. From October 1952 a three shilling (15p) fare was introduced on the bus service.

During the 1951/52 winter the Belfast service routed via Manchester and the Jersey service was suspended. A service to Glasgow via Manchester was inaugurated on 20 April 1952, operated thrice weekly. It was poorly timed for Midlands businessmen. Travel time between Birmingham and Scotland was reduced to two hours on 19 April 1953, though, when a Pionair (modified Dakota) Glasgow-Edinburgh-Birmingham-Northolt service opened.

In July 1952 Aer Lingus operated a Bristol 170 Wayfarer into Elmdon on its scheduled services; in February four Wayfarers brought in sixteen racehorses from Dublin for the Cheltenham races. Twenty-two passengers and three crew had a miraculous escape on 1 January 1953 when the inbound Dakota EI-ACF crashlanded in a field at Spernal Heath, near Alcester. The Viscount was introduced on the Dublin route in July 1954, cutting flight time to fifty minutes.

To the chagrin of local residents but the delight of coach operators, Elmdon has often been a major diversionary airport. One of the first occasions was when London suffered its infamous smog of December 1952. Fifteen flights, with 400 passengers, some from Dublin, Oslo and Aberdeen, passed through.

Air France operated its first scheduled DC-4 service to Elmdon (from Paris) in April 1953, but runway limitations caused the aircraft to be flown 15,000 lb below its normal loaded weight.

The Automobile Association organised an experimental flight on 7 May 1953 from Birmingham to Le Touquet using a Silver City Airways Bristol Superfreighter, which took two cars, two motorcycles and eighteen passengers there in ninety minutes. This was with a view to operating a regular ferry service to the Continent the next year. Such a service was opened by Silver City in June 1955. However, because of poor support, this daily service lasted only until August. Silver City operated to the Isle of Man in 1956, perhaps in 1957 and certainly in 1958 and 1961.

Eric Scott was succeeded as Airport Commandant in July 1953 by J A Gordon AFC, who previously had managed Gatwick and Stansted.

Another independent airline to appear at Elmdon in 1953 was Derby Aviation, which opened a scheduled Derby - Wolverhampton - Jersey route, with a call at Birmingham for customs clearance, on 18 July. The first service was operated with Rapide G-AEAL with Capt E W A Lines in command. This summer service also operated in 1954. Dakotas were introduced

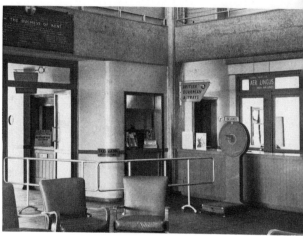

Top: The terminal forecourt, circa 1950.
Centre: The entrance to the Elmdon terminal, about 1950.
Below: Birmingham Air Terminal, circa 1951. (all Negus Collection)

on the route on 6 May 1955. A Derby - Birmingham - Ostend route, operated using the Dakota G-ANTD and the 20-seat Marathon G-AMGW, opened on 7 May 1956.

During 1953 BEA started operating Airspeed Ambassadors, which it called Elizabethans, on an occasional basis, replacing Dakotas. On 5 October 1953 Elizabethans took over the Manchester-Birmingham-Paris route. The shortness of the runway prevented BEA from operating the type with full loads out of Elmdon. The first Elizabethan flight to Paris was by G-ALZX, commanded by Capt G McLannahan, with seventeen passengers from Manchester and thirty-eight from Birmingham.

BEA chopped and changed its schedules out of Birmingham with the changing of the seasons in the 1950s. From 4 October 1953 it doubled its frequency to Heathrow and that month improved its timings to Scotland so one could fly to Edinburgh and Aberdeen and return that evening. Day return services to Belfast (via Manchester) began in April 1954. On 11 April 1954 Viscounts came on the daily London service and also the Manchester - Birmingham - Paris run (first flight by Capt Holman). However, on the same day and with little warning, Air France closed its Birmingham operation, citing the city's proximity to London as the reason. It was to be many years before another Continental airline operated scheduled services to the city. It was widely thought that Air France feared that the turbo-prop Viscount would show up the age of its DC-4s. After all, the Viscount cut flight time to Paris to seventy-five minutes - nearly half an hour less than the Elizabethan and virtually an hour less than the Dakota

In the summer of 1953 the fast-growing independent Eagle Aviation applied to operate from Birmingham to Nice, Brussels, and to Dublin and Shannon. In March 1954 it failed to get licences for routes to fifteen European destinations, to be operated with Vikings. However, it did secure a licence for all-cargo services to Dusseldorf, Frankfurt, Copenhagen, Stavanger, Oslo, Stockholm and Gothenburg.

Left, top to bottom:
Don Everall's Rapide G-AGLR takes on passengers. It crashed in October 1956. (Len Bracey)
Silver City Bristol 170 G-AIFV taxies to its stand. (Ron Thairs)
Elizabethan (Airspeed Ambassador) G-AMAA. The fact that the Ensign and the BEA flag are being flown from the cockpit causes one to speculate as to whether this was a special flight. (Negus Collection)
Air France DC-4 F-BBDH parked on the eastern side of the terminal. (B'ham Post & Mail)

Above: BEA's Sikorsky S-51 G-AJOV over Elmdon: the Aer Lingus Dakota is EI-ACT. (BEA 2887)
Below: Sikorsky S-51 G-AJOR at the Hay Mills 'Rotorstation'. (British Airways 3542)

Air Kruise (Kent) Ltd opened a weekly service from Ramsgate (Manston) in June 1954 using Herons and Rapides, but it was short-lived.

The first trans-Atlantic airliner arrived on 22 December 1954: a Sabena DC-4 from New York, Gander and Shannon, to collect 4½ tons of oil heaters made in Willenhall and take them to Brussels.

Don Everall opened a summer service in May 1955 to the Isle of Wight, using Rapides. On 7 October 1956 their Rapide G-AGLR, on a charter flight from Paris to Birmingham with eight passengers, crash-landed near Berkswell. The aircraft caught fire and was gutted but the pilot and passengers escaped unhurt. The pilot and the company were prosecuted for various breaches of regulations.

On the BEA front, the Viscount was achieving instant popularity and stimulating traffic, but connections to Glasgow were widely criticised. During the 1954/55 winter the London service was suspended but a twice weekly Jersey schedule maintained. The Paris service originated from Birmingham (not Manchester) from the summer of 1955. A twice weekly night service to Zurich commenced on 16 June 1955, followed on 23 April 1956 by a Manchester - Birmingham - Dusseldorf Viscount service (first service by G-AMOD, Capt Preston). The Dusseldorf run was operated on Mondays and Wednesdays by Viscounts (flying time 105 minutes) and on Tuesdays, Thursdays and Sundays by Pionairs (160 minutes). Also on 23 April the Russian leaders Bulganin and Krushchev flew in on a scheduled BEA Viscount flight to visit the British Industries Fair. A weekly freight service to London, operated on Thursday evenings, began in April 1956 but survived only a few months.

BEA helicopters reappeared in 1956 for a new Birmingham-Leicester-Nottingham service, operated thrice daily from 2 July, and later twice daily. Westland-Sikorsky S-55s were used. By the time the route was withdrawn, on 10 November, 1,829 passengers had used it and an 84% regularity achieved.

The first cargo flight to the United States from Elmdon was on 6 August 1955 by an Airwork Ltd DC-4. It went to New York via Manchester, Prestwick and Montreal. However, this twice-weekly (Wednesdays and Saturdays) service lasted only until December. The airline blamed government indifference for its failure. Airwork continued twice-weekly flights to Dusseldorf and Frankfurt, though, until March 1956.

In April 1957 Don Everall bought the Dakota G-ANEG. It operated the lion's share of the scheduled services in 1958, not to mention Inclusive Tour (IT) flights to Palma, Perpignan and Basel. A second Dakota, G-AMSF, joined in 1959, enabling more European holiday destinations to be served from Birmingham. Derby Airways had also spotted the new IT market and on 18 May 1957 operated its first Birmingham - Palma IT service for Midland Air Tour Operators (MATO), with a Dakota commanded by Capt Lines. The Wolverhampton call on the Jersey service ceased in 1957 and from 1958 it was no longer necessary to call for customs clearance at Birmingham on flights to Jersey, although return flights still had to. Four flights a week operated to Ostend in 1958.

Eagle planned to open a twice-weekly route to Palma on 29 March 1958, with a refuelling stop at Blackbushe. A Viscount 800 flew in on a demonstration flight on 19 February, but on 28 March Eagle was told that the Spanish Government had withdrawn its consent. They later relented to the extent of allowing a weekly Viking IT flight (a visit by Eagle's Viking G-AIHA on 7 June was noted as being unusual, prompting one to wonder if it operated the first service), but only with rigorous conditions attached. It has also been reported, though, that Viscount G-APDX operated to Palma that summer.

The post-Suez petrol shortage compelled BEA to suspend its Zurich and London services for periods in early 1957. It joined Aer Lingus on the Dublin route from 15 April after the expiry of the Anglo-Irish Air Agreement, but only with Pionairs (Dakotas). That summer saw a big expansion of the Corporation's services out of Elmdon. At last a direct Glasgow connection was possible and more Viscounts operated to Dusseldorf. Traffic to the Channel Isles grew healthily. Alas, the Dusseldorf service was poorly supported and was withdrawn in the autumn. The BEA summer 1958 programme was virtually an all-Viscount affair, with Pionairs serving only Belfast and the Channel Islands from Birmingham.

Debates and controversy about runways litter the story of Elmdon. In 1953 Birmingham Corporation strongly urged the Government to extend the main runway so as to stimulate new services and not prevent BEA from introducing the Viscount to the city. In early 1954 the Ministry of Civil Aviation approved runway strengthening to enable Elizabethans and Viscounts with full loads to use it. But when work finally got under way in late 1958 to extend it by 800 feet there was a sting in the tail - BEA promptly withdrew all its Continental (Viscount) services, saying the construction work precluded use of the turboprop. To sugar the pill, it laid on a second Pionair frequency to Heathrow to connect with flights from there to Europe. The Viscounts - in fact the larger series

Above: Midland Aero Club Tiger Moths on a Sunday morning in 1958. G-ANLB, nearest camera, was damaged beyond repair at Southam, Warwickshire, 17 March 1962; G-AOEL was owned by W A Holland at Elmdon from 1959; G-AOHY was used as spares in 1960.
Below: BEA Sikorsky S-55 departs for Leicester, July 1956. (British Airways 5496)

802 and 806 aircraft - reappeared when the extension opened on 1 June 1959 and operations to Paris, Dusseldorf and Zurich resumed .

Derby Aviation operated IT flights in 1959 on behalf of MATO to Perpignan and Nice, and on behalf of Lords Brothers on the exotic route to Gatwick, Jersey, Biarritz, Madrid, Marrakesh, Agadir, Tenerife, Agadir again, Tangier, and back. This Dakota-operated tour operated from 10 Actober. In the same year a Birmingham - Oslo IT licence was secured.

In 1959 Birmingham Corporation considered opening a heliport at Calthorpe Park. Fison Airwork Ltd was interested in operating a Battersea Heliport - Birmingham service using twelve-seat S-55s. This scheme came to nothing. Hopes that BEA would re-open helicopter routes from the city were dashed in September 1962, when the Corporation was told by BEA that they simply were not an economic proposition.

Also in 1959 Aer Lingus introduced the Fokker F.27 Friendship on its Dublin run, trimming five minutes off the flight time.

During the late 1950s many aircraft on test or training flights came to use Elmdon's new Instrument Landing System (but often did not actually land). These included many Bristol Britannias on pre-delivery trials, including El Al's 4X-AGC on 10 November 1957; BOAC's G-AOVG, 'VH, 'VI and 'VJ on 25 January and 6, 16 and 27 February 1958 respectively; Canadian Pacific's CF-CZA and 'ZX on 14 February and 21 June 1958 respectively, and G-ANCD, destined for Northeast Airlines, on 19 March 1958. Argosies, fresh from the Bitteswell factory, were another familiar sight. Aircraft coming for overhaul by Fields Aircraft Services at Wymeswold in Leicestershire, many of them Dakotas from far afield, often cleared customs at Elmdon. The ILS system was also used extensively by light aircraft from the training school at Kidlington, Oxford and new Pipers assembled at Oxford by CSE Aviation on test. Piper Apaches, and later Beech Barons from the College of Air Training, Hamble, and RAF aircraft, notably Varsities from Little Rissington. Later, Dominies and Jetstreams from Finningley and various transport aircraft from Brize Norton and Lyneham were to be seen.

Below: BEA Viscount 802 G-AOHI taxies out - possibly on an inaugural service, if the film camera on the terminal verandah has any significance, leaving Dakota G-ALLI.

Elmdon's Swinging Sixties

The most significant development for the airport in the early 1960s was its return to the city on 1 April 1960. The first serious political soundings about returning Elmdon to local authority control were in 1953. The Council was anxious, though, that agreement be reached with the Ministry of Civil Aviation so that ratepayers would not be saddled with the full operating cost of the airport. The transfer was approved by Birmingham City Council early in 1959. The Ministry of Civil Aviation (now the Civil Aviation Authority) contributed 60% of the cost of approved capital projects in excess of £1,000. J A Gordon, Commandant since 1953, kept both his job and its military-sounding title and H K Jackson, formerly Clerk to the Airport Committee, became Manager.

Ten thousand people attended the ceremony on 2 April at which the City formally took back control and officially renamed Elmdon as Birmingham Airport. A display was held, including Bevereley XH116, an Argosy, Gannet WN353, a Canberra, Varsity WJ918, Jet Provost, Vampire XJ775, Wessex helicopter, Dove G-AKJG and Heron G-ANPV of Tube Investments and Westland Widgeon helicopter G-APTE.

At a celebratory lunch at the Council House, Airport Committee chairman Councillor Vic Turton outlined plans to spend £200,000 on better facilities.

On 28 April 1961 HRH The Duchess of Kent, who it will be remembered had opened the airport in 1939, returned to open officially an extension to the terminal for international flights. This had been agreed to by the Government in November 1957 and cost £190,000.

Other improvements made in the early 1960s included increased car parking, better restaurant facilities, the installation of Precision Approach Radar and a £187,000 apron extension. A multi-storey car park was built in 1965.

But while passenger figures improved dramatically during this period - there were 50% more passengers in 1960 than in 1959 - the Corporation had to learn the hard way that improved airport facilities do not necessarily result in more airlines and routes.

Don Everall's Dakota G-AMSF was written off in a spectacular fashion on 5 March 1960. Members of Moseley Rugby Club were among the twenty-eight passengers who had a miraculous escape when their Jersey-bound aircraft swerved just after take-off and crashed. The Dakota missed a hangar by a few feet and the starboard wing scraped along the runway until the propellers churned into the grass and the fuselage came to rest on its side. Vickers Viking G-AKBG was delivered to Everall on 18 May 1960, followed by G-AMNK on 25 May. But G-AMNK was lost off Crete on 24 August whilst on a cargo charter. Don Everall's airline division was bought by Gatwick-based Air Safaris in November and Mr Everall made a director. The last

Below: 47 Squadron's Beverley XH116, coded 'Y', attracts the crowds, 2 April 1960. (Birmingham Post & Mail)

Above: Vampire XJ775 and Gannet WN353 at the hand-over display, 2 April 1960. (Airport Collection)

Left: Varsity WJ918, coded 'F' at the same event, 2 April 1960. (Trefor Jones)

Below: Elmdon in about 1960. The new international terminal is under construction. (Airport Collection)

revenue flight by its remaining Dakota, G-ANEG, was on 2 January 1961. Don Everall's light aviation activities continued at Wolverhampton until that airport closed in 1970.

Air Safaris inherited Everall's scheduled routes from Birmingham to Exeter, Guernsey, Jersey and the Isle of Man and also an unused Birmingham - Newcastle licence. There were also IT licences to Basel, Malaga, Nice, Perpignan and Rimini. The airline opened the Newcastle route on 3 June 1961 using Viking G-AHOW. During the winter of 1960/61 Air Safaris flew various charters to Dublin and Paris. In 1961 summer services were opened to Jersey (27 May), Guernsey (1 July) and Sandown (using a leased North-South Airlines Heron on 3 June). IT flights were flown by Hermes and Viking aircraft. In 1961 these were principally to Copenhagen, Perpignan, Stavanger and Nice. Financial problems led to a general curbing of operations, manifested by the withdrawal of the Bournemouth - Birmingham - Newcastle route after Viking G-AGRS operated it on 4 September. The airline's last services were on 31 October 1961 and in January 1962 its licences were revoked.

Other independents evident at this time included Overseas Aviation, which in 1961 operated IT flights with Canadair Argonauts to Palma, Valencia and Rimini. The following year's IT season saw Euravia Constellations flying to Palma, Perpignan, Valencia and Rimini and Lloyd International DC-4s serving Palma, Venice and Naples. Euravia served Venice and Naples again in 1963, and was renamed Britannia Airways in 1964. European aircraft on IT flights started making their mark in 1964; Aviaco DC-6s from Palma, Societa Aerea Mediterranea DC-6Bs from Rimini and Airnautic DC-6s from Nice. Between 1961 and 1964 the number of seats offered from the airport on IT flights nearly trebled.

The Eagle service to Palma set a new record for Elmdon in July 1960 when a DC-6 disembarked the largest number of people from one aircraft yet - 102 passengers and six crew. In 1961 Cunard Eagle, as it had become, was

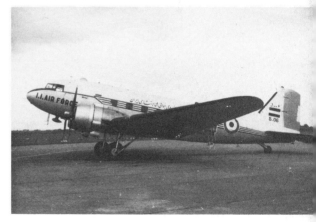

Right, top to bottom:

Model of the international terminal opened in 1961, distinguished by two lovely Dinky toy models of Viscounts - no doubt collector's items today! (Airport Collection)

Ghana Airways Dakota 9G-AAE clears customs at Elmdon, 23 August 1960, en route to Field's at Wymeswold for overhaul. (Neil Lewis)

Another customer for Wymeswold: Imperial Iranian Air Force Dakota 5.06 (Neil Lewis)

Aer Lingus F.27 Friendship EI-AKE at Elmdon.

Top: HRH The Duchess of Kent returned on 28 April 1961 to open the new International Terminal. She is seen with the Lord Mayor, Alderman Garnet Broughton, and the Chairman of the Airport Committee, Cllr Victor Turton.

Below: The terminal forecourt, shortly after the international building (on the left) was opened. (Trefor Jones)

Bottom: In 1960 the floorspace in the original terminal building was increased by building an extension under the eastern canopy. It is seen here just after completion. (Trefor Jones)

licensed to operate to Nice, but decided to postpone the opening for another year as the runway was unsuitable for the Britannias it proposed to use. Despite vehement BEA objections, permission was given in June 1962 for the number of flights on the summer-only twice-weekly service to Palma to become unlimited.

On 4 June 1960 Starways Dakota G-AMSN opened a service to Newquay (St Mawgan) in Cornwall. From 11 June to mid-September North-South operated a Birmingham - Sandown service using Heron G-AOZN. Despite objections from British Railways, Morton Air Services secured permission to operate to Swansea. The route was inaugurated on 1 August 1961, using a Heron which made the trip in fifty-five minutes. On 6 April 1962 Aer Lingus opened a service to the new airport at Cork, using Friendships with a flight time of ninety minutes. At some time between 1961 and October 1964 Mercury operated to Exeter.

Meanwhile, BEA plodded on. On 1 April 1960 it opened a Manchester - Birmingham - Barcelona night summer service. It was an economic disaster - the first five services carried a total of only thirty passengers from Birmingham - one flight did not pick up a single passenger. Yet an additional frequency was scheduled from early 1962. BEA persisted with the route until 1966, when it warned it was under scrutiny - one day that summer the seventy-seat Viscount had only one passenger to Barcelona, and none back. It was finally withdrawn in October 1967.

After intensive lobbying over a period of years by the Council and the local business community, BEA opened a twice-weekly service to Amsterdam in July 1960. Its fare, £19 return, and its timings were considered competitive and the route was given a lavish launch. Early traffic figures were better than for any previous European route from Birmingham - just as well, because this was the first not to originate from Manchester from its inauguration. But this still meant only a 30% load factor. Not only was the route maintained through the following winter but it was increased to five flights weekly. But this was more a political than a commercial gesture. Only two months later BEA's Chief Executive, Anthony Milward, told the Council that the Amsterdam route could not operate with only six passengers on each flight, and must be cut to twice weekly. 'It is the easiest way of losing money that I have ever come across', he said.

KLM applied unsuccessfully to fly the route in 1961. BOAC objected on the grounds that the Dutch airline would use it to generate demand for long distance routes out of Amsterdam. The BEA service was withdrawn at the end of summer 1961. Milward said, 'Birmingham has only itself to blame. Only 17% of the seats were filled last winter and 30% this summer. We need 65% to make the service economic'. BEA later approached KLM to operate the route jointly but the Dutch airline declined on the grounds that it did not then have the right aircraft for the job. BEA reintroduced the Amsterdam service, despite all it had said in the past, on 5 April 1966, operated on Tuesdays and Thursdays. But even the inaugural service carried only thirteen passengers each way. This was blamed on unappealing timings.

There was better news about the Channel Isles routes, which were fully booked in the summer of 1960. During the first eight months of that year there were 198,317 passengers, compared with 126,730 during the same period of 1959. Viscounts cut the flight time to Jersey when they took over the route in summer 1960. Channel Isles routes were suspended, though, during the 1962/63 winter. From 1960 BEA operated 'honeymoon specials' to Jersey, which were often fully booked.

The last regular BEA scheduled Pionair service to Birmingham was on 31 October 1960, from Heathrow. G-AGZB was flown in by Capt Peter Griffin. The aircraft ran off the end of the runway when landing at Elmdon in fog, though, so the last southbound Pionair departure was cancelled.

Despite objections from British United Airways and Cunard Eagle, BEA opened a Manchaster - Birmingham - Milan weekly service on 21 April 1961. It became twice-weekly from 21 June. Traffic on the route was abysmal - on the first flight, the crew outnumbered the passengers, one from Manchester and one from Birmingham. The service was withdrawn in 1964. The loss-making weekly service to Zurich was scrapped at the same time. A rarely mentioned facet of BEA's operations is the weekly IT flight to Basel it operated in 1961 with Viscount 701s and in 1962-64 with Viscount 802s.

In 1962 the Belfast service was routed via Liverpool and the Dusseldorf run stepped up

Right, top to bottom:
Air Safaris Viking G-AJBX at Elmdon. Behind the scaffolding to the left the new glass front to the terminal is being put in. (Delwyn Griffiths)
SAS Convair 440 OY-KPE. (Ron Thairs)
July 1961 was distinguished by the daily visit for a week of the Yugoslav (Jugoslovenki Aerotransport) Dakota YU-ACD, operating to Belgrade with a big consignment of Triumph motorcycles.
Ind Coope's Dove 2 G-APCZ. (Neil Lewis)

from four to five flights weekly. The Vanguard first visited Birmingham in August 1962. It was the largest type yet to visit the airport and could not depart with a full load because the main runway was too short. BEA stressed that this visit did not signal Vanguard services out of Birmingham in the near future.

During the 1962/63 winter, the morning departure to London was brought forward from 0845 to 0800 to give better connections at Heathrow and the well-used service to Glasgow supplemented by a third flight, via Manchester. The sales shop in New Street opened in August 1963. Demand for seats to Glasgow justified 'doubling up' some departures by January 1964 - operating a second aircraft ten minutes later. This was the only option, as larger aircraft could not operate profitably out of Elmdon.

Stand-by fares, already a feature on BEA's services from Heathrow to Belfast and Scotland, were introduced on the Heathrow - Birmingham run from 1 November 1963. The stand-by fare of £1-13s (£1.65) compared with a normal single fare of £2-10s (£2.50) and a second-class rail fare of £1-7s-9d (£1.34).

A service to Edinburgh opened on 1 November 1965, but businessmen could only put in a day's work there if they flew via Glasgow in the morning. A mid-morning service to Glasgow commenced in May 1966. The first BEA Vanguard services appear to have been during Whitsun and the seamen's strike of 1966, to the Channel Isles.

Cargo traffic in and out of Birmingham suffered as shippers turned to using the new motorways. An improved 28,000 sq ft freight terminal at Elmdon opened on 1 April 1968, in a hangar, but there was a steady trend towards taking goods to London for onward carriage.

On the independent front, Executive Air Transport was founded by Capt Eric Ashton DFC, who previously flew a Dove for Tarmac, with Jack Muldoon, former Chief Flying Instructor with the Midland Aero Club, and Mr Mole, who owned Enstone aerodrome. The name of the company was devised by Muldoon. Mole bought the Piper Tri-Pacer G-ARBS for £3,000 but then the major prospective client said he did not want to use single-engined aircraft. Ashton introduced Capt Alan Firmin, former local manager of Air Safaris, as Commercial Manager. The group then met G Roland Dawes, Chairman of Neville Industrial Developments Ltd, who was interested in backing and using them. Dawes bought the Dove G-AMDD as a hack in December 1960, then chartered it out. In April 1961 the Dakota G-ANEG was acquired, which was often chartered by Derby Airways. In October 1961 Executive Air Transport applied to take over North-South's unused

licence to Leeds/Bradford, using Doves, Herons or Dakotas. After the demise of Air Safaris, Executive secured the licences to operate to Newcastle (opened with G-ANEG on 3 April 1962) and Sandown. The Sandown route, via Bournemouth, was to be operated with Herons four times weekly from 22 May, but it never materialised. Instead, on 9 May, the Sandown and Newcastle licences were transferred to Derby Airways. Executive also sold its subsidiary, Midland Airport Services Ltd, to Derby Airways for only £100. It handled various airlines' flights at Elmdon, including those of Euravia, Lloyd International, Dan-Air, Autair, Starways, Morton Air Services. In December 1962 it took over from BEA the handling of Aer Lingus flights. Firmin set up Executive Air Engineering at Coventry.

Derby Airways, meanwhile, operated a Derby - Birmingham - Cork schedule from 22 December 1961 through the Christmas and New Year period and again in summer 1962. Permission for the summer service to Ostend to call at Cambridge, provided passengers did not travel between the British airports, was obtained in 1962. Herons (leased from Mercury Airlines Ltd) were operated on Wednesdays to Sandown from late May 1962. Mercury Herons were also chartered to fly the Newcastle service weekly, on Wednesdays, from 8 May. The first flight was by G-ANCI. Over the winter of 1962/63 services to the Channel Isles were operated. On 2 April 1963 the Newcastle service was stepped up to three services a week, Dakota G-AMSX operating the first service on the new schedule.

During the summer 1963 IT season Derby operated Argonauts to Barcelona, Cork, Ostend, Palma, Perpignan, Rimini, Tarbes, Valencia and Venice and Dakotas on some Ostend services. On 8 August Argonauts G-ALHG and 'HY took 150 children to Poitiers. By this time Derby Airways carried out some Argonaut maintenance in the hangars at Birmingham.

In June 1964 Derby Airways obtained permission to fly from Derby and Birmingham to

Right: Top to bottom:

Euravia's Constellation G-AHEN starts its take-off run. (Trefor Jones)

Another Constellation. This is Skyway's G-ANUR. (Trefor Jones)

In 1961 KLM's Super Constellation PH-LKN brought in a 6-ton turbo-blower from Canada for repair by AEI at Rugby. The Connie ousted the DC-6 as the largest aircraft to have used the airport. (Ron Thairs)

The first pure jet airliner to visit Elmdon was the RAF Transport Command Comet XK716 'Cepheus' on 18 April 1961.

Blackpool, but said it was unlikely to open the service that year. IT destinations in 1964 were Barcelona, Genoa, Ibiza, Ostend, Perpignan, Valencia and Venice. The airline was renamed British Midland Airways on 1 October in anticipation of moving base from Burnaston to the new East Midlands Airport. A scheduled Derby - Birmingham - Amsterdam freight service opened on 6 October but was withdrawn in January 1965 after making heavy losses. During the summer of 1965 scheduled services from Birmingham to Newcastle, Ostend and Sandown were flown.

In early 1962 Solair Flying Services was formed as an off-shoot of the Taberrer Travel Agency, Solihull. It operated charter, aerial photography and pleasure flights from Elmdon and Baginton using the Rapides G-AHKV and 'LBC. However, G-ALBC crashed in Derbyshire on 30 December 1963 whilst returning from a photographic assignment. Licences to operate from Birmingham and Baginton to the Isles of Scilly via either Exeter or Staverton were received in June 1964. It was intended to open these routes on 27 June, but for reasons unknown they were only partially operated, from 3 July, using Cessna 172C G-ARWP. Solair's flying activity dwindled during September and ceased on 4 October.

Another small operator born at Elmdon was Mid-Fly Ltd, in April 1964. Two Piper Colts, G-ARKK and 'KO, formed the equipment of a flying school from 22 September. They were later joined by Tri-Pacer G-ARHS. The Managing Director was M J Webb, General Manager E J Bott and chief pilot Capt C C Holloway. An air taxi service was offered after Apache G-APCL was bought in November. Photographic and pleasure work was also carried out. Solair's Rapide G-AHKV was bought in February 1965, to be joined in March by Rapide G-AJKW. But both Rapides were under-utilised and sold in 1966. Piper Aztec G-ARYF was busier - it arrived on 15 March 1965 and flew to ten other UK airports and Copenhagen in its first month. In 1966 Mid-Fly set up Birmingham Air Centre, which offered Cessna 150s and Piper Colts for training. After Mid-Fly was taken over by Air Gregory in January 1969 it was renamed Air Gregory (Mid-Fly) Ltd. The new owners took over the air taxi work for themselves and the emphasis was placed on air training at Coventry.

Early in 1961 the energetic Councillor Turton, Chairman of the Airport Committee, announced that capital was being sought to enable the main (16/34) runway to be extended to 7,000 feet. He hoped that this would make Birmingham a prime diversion airport for Heathrow and more suitable for direct flights to Europe. He thought the extension would suffice for the decade or so before VTOL aircraft made runways obsolete!

It was at this time that residents of Marston Green began to protest against further airport development, principally because of the noise. They were particularly annoyed by the ground running of engines at night. The disturbance caused by a BOAC VC-10 on 31 August 1964 using the Instrument Landing System for familiarisation, and the diversion of seven Viscounts, two Ambassadors and an Argosy on 12 December could not have improved tempers.

The relative merits of extending the runway (from 5,006 feet) to 7,000 feet at a cost of £650,000, or to 7,500 feet for £1.15 million, were considered by the Airport Committee in 1962. A delegation to BOAC lobbying for transAtlantic services from Birmingham was told that the city should get itself a 10,000 foot runway - double its existing length. The urgency of the problem was emphasised by Anthony Milward of BEA in September when he warned that Birmingham's future inclusion in their route network would be jeopardised if it could not handle Vanguards and Tridents.

Left: Evocative view of the Rolls-Royce Merlin 626 engines of a Derby Airways Argonaut on the apron at Elmdon. (Trefor Jones)

At the end of 1962 it was resolved to extend to 7,400 feet at a total cost of £650,000. This was subject to Ministry of Aviation approval, as 60% of the money would come from the Government. Despite vehement opposition from the Marston Green Residents Association, Ministry of Aviation approval was received in 1963. The Public Enquiry into the extension sat from 17 to 31 December 1963 and final approval given on 7 July 1964.

Delays caused by the Public Enquiry caused the cost to increase by about £425,000 and further wrangling about who should pay this further postponed construction work. Jet services began after 300 feet of the extension had been completed in the spring of 1966. Between April and September 1966 about 300 jet flights were scheduled, for example by British United BAC One-Elevens and Spantax SA Convair 990A Coronados.

In order to encourage new routes, the Airport Committee considered reducing landing fees by a third in 1962 for airlines opening new services. The Ministry of Aviation, which fixed all landing fees, indicated some sympathy for the idea. One Councillor argued, however, that it would be a dangerous precedent and might increase the burden on ratepayers.

On several occasions in the early 1960s Councillor Turton claimed that European airlines, including Sabena, Lufthansa, Swissair, SAS and Alitalia, wanted to fly to Birmingham. Only KLM had made an official application, however. Turton attempted to have Birmingham declared an 'international free airport' in 1962, with no restrictions on foreign airlines. This was flatly rejected.

A delegation from Birmingham to Peter Thorneycroft, Minister of Aviation, was told there was little hope of the British state airlines expanding their services from the city, and suggested that the independents should be approached.

Accordingly, Turton met Freddie Laker, then Managing Director of British United Airways, in October 1963. Laker promised to consider operating out of Birmingham. At this time he was contesting with BEA the right to operate

Right, top to bottom:

Swissair Convair Cv.440 Metropolitan HB-IML. (Ron Thairs)

Aeromaritime's DC-6B F-BGSN at Elmdon, apparently on charter to Land-Rover, and Chipmunk G-AOFF. About 1960. (Ron Thairs)

RAF Anson VM369 makes a brief stop on 20 June 1961. (Neil Lewis)

Transair Sweden's Curtiss C-46 SE-EDR, early 1960s. (Trefor Jones)

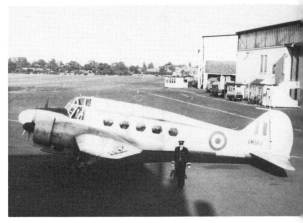

from Birmingham to Genoa. Eventually, British United announced the first pure-jet scheduled service from Birmingham, via Gatwick to Genoa, to start in 1965. On 28 January a demonstration flight from Gatwick with a BAC One-Eleven was aborted after hydraulic trouble developed. In August BUA operated a scheduled service to the Isle of Man.

Turton meanwhile tried to tempt Coventry Council with an offer to share the running of Birmingham Airport. Coventry had recently failed to get permission to extend Baginton's runway, but nevertheless could not be won over. They were adamant that the development of Elmdon should not stunt the growth of Baginton. This partisan approach seems short-sighted compared with that of the councils in the East Midlands who were jointly developing the airport at Castle Donington.

The Council criticised British Eagle in 1965 when it decided to drop the summer route to Newquay which it had secured after buying the Liverpool-based airline Starways, having promised to keep Starways' routes active. In May 1967 British Eagle introduced BAC One-Elevens to Newquay and Palma and in May 1968 on a new Liverpool - Birmingham - Ibiza weekly service. British Eagle also held a Birmingham - Nice licence, but never used it. On 7 November 1968, though, it ceased trading and went into liquidation the next day.

Over the years many firms have acquired their own aircraft for the transportation of executives and urgent goods. The speed, convenience, flexibility and security for a company in having its own fleet can more than justify the cost. Corporate operators at Elmdon have included Tube Investments, which moved in with a Rapide in 1954, first to occupy No 3 hangar and later No 1. From September 1958 it operated Dove G-AKJG, from October 1959 Heron G-ANPV and from 1970, just before the Heron was sold, Beech King Air G-AYLW. On 18 May 1978 it acquired Super King Air G-BKTI, to replace G-AYLW which left in November 1978. G-BKTI was disposed of in 1981.

J C Bamford, the Rocester earth-moving equipment manufacturers, based Dove G-ARJB, named 'Exporter I' at Elmdon from September 1960 and Dove G-APVX 'Exporter II' from March 1969 to January 1971. Its HS.125 Srs 400B jet G-AYLI 'Exporter III' was delivered on 22 December 1970. JCB moved its aircraft to East Midlands Airport in 1971.

BSR Ltd based their Dove G-ASMG at Birmingham from November 1963 to February 1965. HS.125 Srs.1 G-ASSM was delivered on 19 February 1965 and flew to the USA on a sales trip in June. It was sold in 1970. An HS.125 Srs.400B, G-AXDM, was delivered to BSR on 30 October 1969 and operated until August 1970. JetRanger helicopter G-AVTE was used for a time from February 1968 to commute between Elmdon and BSR's factory at Old Hill.

GKN's Aviation Department began when the Vandervell Company, which owned Dove G-ANGU, was taken over in 1967. It was based at Coventry until November 1970, when it moved to Birmingham with Queen Air G-AWOI, which it disposed of in 1971, and Islander G-AXXG, which stayed until 1981. HS.125 Srs.1B/R.522 G-ATWH was bought from Granada Television by GKN Birfield Transmissions Ltd in April 1970 and transferred to GKN Group Services Ltd in December 1971; it was retained until 1976. From 25 October 1971 to 1981 King Air G-AXFE was operated; Bolkow 105D helicopter G-BCRG served from November 1974 to 1980 and HS.125 Srs.600B from 11 May 1976 to 1981. Currently the only GKN-owned aircraft at Birmingham is the Beechcraft 200 Super King Air G-GKNB, acquired in March 1980.

Private flying has continued at Elmdon, despite the demands on space and air traffic control by commercial and corporate aviation. The cost of basing a light aeroplane here would generally be greater than at a specialist light aviation field - but then, of course, the pilot would not have access to all the facilities taken for granted at Birmingham - twenty-four opening and ILS to name but two! For many years Arthur Harrison was a leading local pilot, with his Auster 5 G-ALFA and later Aero 145 G-AROE. Eric F Allchin owned a succession of aeroplanes: Prentice G-AOKO (based from June 1959 to August 1963), Auster 5 G-AOTJ (from 1959), Cherokee 160 G-ARVT (from 1963 to February 1968), Cherokee 235 G-ASLV (delivered 4 September 1964, kept until 1965), Comanche 260 G-ATAO (from 1965 to March 1968), Twin Comanche 160 G-AVVI (delivered 19 October 1966, sold in October 1971) and Twin Comanche G-AYZE (May 1971 to July 1973). Mr Allchin's last aircraft was the Beechcraft Baron G-AZUJ, acquired in July 1972, in which he and three others died when it crashed landing in fog at night at Birmingham on 29 November 1975. Arthur Penzer, a founder and Chief Flying Instructor of the Warwickshire Aero Club, was the co-pilot.

The first Russian-built aircraft to land at Elmdon was the Antonov AN-12 CU-T827 of Cubana de Aviacion, with two Proteus engines for overhaul by Bristol Siddeley at Coventry, on 3 July 1966. The World Cup that year brought Constellation D-ALEM and Douglas DC-7C D-ABAR on 16 July from Hamburg and Cologne.

At last, KLM opened a service from Amsterdam, on 2 November 1966, using a Lockheed Electra - the first type incidentally, to offer

Top: BSR's HS.125 jet G-ASSM

Above: The Midland Aero Club's Aircoupe G-ARXR at Elmdon after its delivery flight from Southampton, 1961. The pilot was Henri Ducommun. Note the reconstruction work on the control tower. (Henri Ducommun)

Right: Not exactly a hectic day. One of the posters behind the check-in desks promotes a new direct BEA London-Tangier service - which means this was probably 1966. (Negus Collection)

Top: Derby Airways Dakota G-AOGZ taxies past a BEA Viscount on to its stand on the international apron. (Delwyn Griffiths)

Above: Cunard Eagle Viscount V.755D G-AOCB no doubt on one of its frequent inclusive-tour services. (Trefor Jones)

Below: One of the hazards of trying to operate an international airport in the British winter weather - a not uncommon sight, snow clearing going on around a BEA Viscount, circa 1962. (Airport Collection)

first class seats on a scheduled service out of Birmingham. From 5 April 1967 Douglas DC-9 jets operated the route - the first scheduled jet service from the city.

BEA's Viscounts operating to Amsterdam and Dusseldorf were converted from 65-seat aircraft to 32-seaters with increased provision for cargo from October 1966. A second daily flight to Edinburgh was added on 1 April 1967 but during 1968/69 the service went via Manchester because of poor support. Vanguards were introduced on the services to London (from 25 March 1967, first service by G-APET) and the Channel Isles (from 15 May), after the runway extension opened. In August 1967 the Council asked for the London service to be increased to three flights daily, but the low load factors did not justify extra flights. BEA jets appeared in June 1968, when Comets opened a new weekly service to Malta (leaving at 0450, prompting further protests about noise) and Tridents replaced Viscounts on some flights to Paris and Glasgow. The first Trident departure to Paris on 1 June was cancelled because of riots there.

1967 was a poor year for BEA at Birmingham. Load factors were 75% to Jersey, 69% to Guernsey, 53% to Glasgow, 49% to London, 58% to Belfast, 56% to Dublin, 38% to Dusseldorf, 36% to Edinburgh and only 27% to Amsterdam. Chairman Sir Anthony Milward wrote in May 1968 that none of the services out of Birmingham was profitable. Yet - despite the notorious load factors on the route - BEA increased its flights to Amsterdam from two to five a week when KLM withdrew in October 1968 because lack of demand.

Flights to Paris were switched from Le Bourget to Orly in April 1969. In July BAC One-Elevens replaced the Tridents on the route. Tridents replaced the Comets on the Glasgow-Birmingham-Malta route on 1 April, allegedly creating much more noise. A JP living in Hall Green is supposed to have told a local paper, 'The windows were shaking and I almost fell out of bed'. One suspects that either the reporter had a gift for inventing quotes or the JP needed a new bed. The equipment was, however, popular with customers. The Trident 3 was introduced on the Malta service on 1 November 1971.

The ten-bedroom Airport Hotel was taken over by Fortes in 1966 and extended. A new block was 'topped out' in July 1968 and on 17 December the new sixty-six-bedroom Excelsior Hotel opened as a joint BEA/Fortes venture. In August 1969 Fortes announced that the new hotel had proved so popular they would spend another £228,000 on expanding it to 140 rooms.

An Air Spain Britannia, operating to Palma for MATO, was the first aircraft to use the run-

Above: British United Viscount 831 G-APNE. (Ron Thairs)

Right: First visit by a BEA Vanguard (G-APEL), 1962.

Below: Apron scene, about 1965. The BEA Viscount G-AOHM (left) is in a short-lived colour scheme in which the registration is below the insignia, not above. The British Midland Viscount is in one of that company's earlier schemes.

Opposite page, top: Work on the runway extension in progress during 1967. (Airport Collection)
Bottom: Aerial view after completion of the runway extension. Note the pre-1942, pre-NEC, pre-Birmingham International Station, pre-1984 airport terminal rural tranquility beyond the airport boundary! (Airport Collection)
This page, above: Survey photo of Elmdon 5 August 1967. An aircraft (a Viscount?) is about to touch down on runway 15. (Airport Collection)

way extension, on 23 March 1967. However, the 7,400 foot runway was not officially opened until 7 April, by Board of Trade President Douglas Jay. To take account of the magnetic shift over the years, the runways were redesignated on 22 March from 16-34 to 15-33 and from 07-25 to 06-24. The first official user of the extended runway was BEA Trident G-ARPC from London, piloted by Capt H S Johnson.

Birmingham's first trans-Atlantic commercial passenger flight was on 3 June, when Caledonian's Britannia G-AOVH from Montreal diverted from Gatwick. From June Air France Caravelles operated a fortnightly charter service to Nice. Caravelles were also used on a summer night scheduled service to Palma by Iberia from 18 August. Elmdon's first Boeing 707 also came in August - G-ASZF of BOAC, chartered by Tube Investments to take almost thirty tons of research equipment to New York. In September Aer Lingus Boeing 707 EI-APG operated a charter to Boston via Shannon (return by EI-AMW on 2 October), while in October a Seaboard DC-8 picked up thirty-four tons of abrasive cloth for Chicago. This was the first of a series of flights - N801SW came in on 6 November and N804SW on 4 December. Autair brought in a BAC One-Eleven in November to demonstrate for travel agents the type that was to carry the bulk of MATO customers the following season. An Aeroflot Ilyushin Il-18T, CCCP-75435, brought members of the Royal Shakespeare Company home from Moscow on 17 December after their triumphant visits to Helsinki, Leningrad and Moscow. Another Aeroflot Il-18 came in 1968 with a party of opticians (- an optical Ilyushin?!)

Not surprisingly, this new jet activity caused a dramatic increase in protests about noise. The news that each passenger passing through Birmingham cost ratepayers only 4 shillings (20p), compared with £3-13s (£3.65) at Coventry and £1-13s (£1.65) at East Midlands, could not have soothed those residents who started a campaign to ring up members of the Airport Committee and the Director whenever they were woken by aircraft.

And was it deprivation of sleep that made Vic Turton dream up 'Birmingham Airways' in 1968? His idea was to lease two BAC One-Elevens from BEA and operate them on schedules determined by the council. The idea came to nothing.

In February 1968 Jack Muldoon set up a charter company with an Aztec, G-AVRX. He wanted to call it Air Executive Ltd, but this was too similar to Executive Air Transport and the day before the official launch Muldoon was obliged to rename his company Air Envoy Ltd. The day of the launch did not go smoothly,

either. Muldoon had asked the Lord Mayor to name the aircraft *City of Birmingham,* but it was stranded by fog at Coventry. Instead, Mid-Fly's Aztec G-ARYF was used for the ceremony. However, the name 'Air Envoy' proved to be too ambiguous - people did not realise it was an air charter company - so Muldoon decided to adopt the name 'Central Air Services'. Its first office was a room above his brother's garage. Despite this inauspicious start, Central Air Services has survived the years. Aircraft that have seen service with the firm include Aztec D G-AYZN, Cessna 337F G-AZAV, Aztec F G-BFKN, Reims Cessna F.152 G-CPFC and Navajo Chieftain G-TROT. Its current fleet consists of Cessna 421C Golden Eagle II G-BEFT, which was bought by Lucas Industries on 21 October 1976 and passed to Eclipsol Ltd in 1981, to be operated by Central, and Cessna 500 Citation G-BHTT, registered on 4 August 1980, operated by Central on behalf of Lucas. In 1969 the Dakota G-AGJV was bought for charter work and use on a weekly Birmingham-Ostend service, but it was immediately leased to Air Ulster and was sold in January 1970 having never operated for Central.

British Eagle's licences for Liverpool-Birmingham-Palma and -Ibiza were taken over by Channel Airways, but it never operated the Palma route and lost its rights to it in February 1970. Thus, when Iberia recommenced its summer Palma service on 1 June 1969, it enjoyed a monopoly on the route. British Midland took over the Birmingham-Newquay licence, but also did not exercise it in 1969. British Midland did, however, open a scheduled winter service to Jersey to replace the BEA one, in October 1968. Soon after, it applied unsuccessfully to compete directly with BEA on its Channel Islands routes. In January 1969 British Midland merged with Invicta Airways and in March BMA's General Manager, Michael Bishop, was made a Director of the Company. These developments mark the beginning of an aggressive rivalry between BMA and the state airline that is still making headlines today.

More jets came in 1969 in the shape of Aer Lingus Boeing 737s, replacing Viscounts on their Dublin service.

On 18 January the first VC-10 landed - BOAC Super VC-10 G-ASGK on a command training flight from Shannon. BOAC's Managing Director, Keith Granville, flew in a VC-10 to Birmingham on 19 August to announce a scheduled, four time weekly, Birmingham-Manchester -New York service from 1970 - an exciting prospect for the next decade.

The sixties closed with, in December, fifty diversions to Birmingham in one weekend, bringing in 3,000 passengers.

Elmdon:
The Seventies

For the summer of 1970, BEA boosted its popular service to Malta from two to three flights weekly and stepped up flights to Dusseldorf from two to five a week. But weekend flights to Paris and the mid-day London service were discontinued. There was now only one flight a day to London - by 1971 the route was losing more than £20,000 a year. Yet, on one occasion, it was operated by Boeing 707. One night in February 1972 fog prevented an aircraft from getting to Birmingham to operate the southbound flight, but some BOAC Boeing 707s had been diverted to the Midlands. So next morning sixty-six people travelled to London in a 146-seat Boeing.

On 1 April 1970 a twice-weekly Manchester-Birmingham-Milan freight service opened, jointly marketed by BEA and Alitalia but using Italian DC-9F jets. A similar, thrice-weekly DC-6 service from Birmingham to Copenhagen began on 3 November 1970, operated by SAS but in conjunction with BEA. DC-9Fs were introduced from June 1971 but soon after, the service was abandoned. BEA attempted an all-cargo Merchantman (converted Vanguard) service to Paris, from 5 May 1971, but it lasted only until August. The Milan freight service died at the end of 1972.

The BOAC Super VC-10 service to New York (via Manchester) was inaugurated using G-ASGA on 28 April 1970. Fifteen passengers on each of the four flights a week out of Elmdon were needed to break even, but by June it was averaging only twelve. As intended originally, the route was withdrawn for the winter in October and resumed in May 1971. Despite a £40,000 advertising campaign, reservations were only half the number thought necessary to make the operation worthwhile. It was withdrawn again from October 1971 to 29 May 1972, but during its third summer it went via Prestwick, not Manchester. In February 1973 BOAC announced that the service would not resume after its winter break. Over three years it had lost £¾ million and only attracted an average of thirteen passengers a flight.

On 7 May 1970 the Britannia Airways Boeing 737 G-AVRO *City of Birmingham* (so named in September 1969 but later it quietly became *Sir Francis Drake*) made its first Birmingham - Palma flight, loaded with Horizon Midlands holidaymakers. Under a £3 million deal, G-AVRO would operate exclusively for Horizon Midlands over the next three years.

Other IT operators evident in the 1970-74 period were Air Spain (DC-8s), Aviaco (Caravelles), Aviogenex (Tupolev Tu-134s), Bavarian Airways (BAC One-Elevens), Balair (DC-6Bs, DC-9s), Braathens-SAFE (Fokker F.28s), British Caledonian (BAC One-Elevens), Channel Air-

Below: BOAC Super VC-10 G-ASGG prepares to taxi off the western apron - circa 1970.

A selection of early 1970s
inclusive tour operators;
opposite: Spantax Coronado
EC-BQA in spring 1971;
Bavaria One Eleven;
BEA Airtours Comet 4B
G-APMD, circa 1971;
Dan-Air's Comet 4 G-APDJ;

On this page: BAC One Eleven
G-AXMJ of the doomed Court
Line on finals, runway 33, 23
February 1974; Monarch
Britannia 309 G-ANCH about
to touch down, 4 July 1971;
Viscount 812 of Channel
Airways, 12 April 1971.
(all S G Richards)

ways (Comets, and a weekly Viscount service to Ostend in 1970), Court Line (formerly Autair, BAC One-Elevens), Donaldson International (Britannias), Inex-Adria (DC-9s), JAT (Caravelles), Monarch (Boeing 720Bs, which operated a weekly charter to Toronto and Vancouver in 1974),Societa Aerea Mediterranea (Caravelles), Spantax SA (Coronados), Trans-Europa (DC-7s, Caravelles) and World Airways (DC-8s).

British Air Services, a BEA subsidiary, in 1970 proposed a network of air commuter services using the nineteen-seat Short Skyliner. A Twin Otter, CF-YFT, was demonstrated at Elmdon on 26 May 1970 in connection with the proposal. Twenty-two provincial centres, including Birmingham and Wolverhampton, would be served and a two-hourly service between and London operated. An application for a Birmingham - Southampton route had already been lodged and some proving flights carried out with a Skyliner when the scheme was scrapped.

British Midland had only one route out of Birmingham during the winter of 1970/71, to Jersey, operated four times a week by Viscount and once by BAC One-Eleven. Its scheduled presence during summer 1971 consisted of a weekly Viscount flight to the Isle of Man on Saturdays. At the end of 1971 BMA was given permission to operate to Jersey all year round, in direct competition with BEA during the summer months. Despite an earlier public statement by BEA that it planned routes from Birmingham to Brussels and Frankfurt, it was BMA that opened to those cities, on 10 April 1972. Their service was via Brussels to Frankfurt and operated on Mondays, Tuesdays and Thursdays. During its first three months, passenger figures were 20% above target, enabling another two flights to be added from 4 September. By the end of 1973 BMA were able to sustain separate services to Brussels and Frankfurt. During the winter of 1972/73 BMA flew five times a week to Jersey. Viscount G-AZLR veered off the runway at Elmdon whilst landing after a positioning flight from Leeds/Bradford on 19 January 1973, after its port undercarriage collapsed. The aircraft returned to service a fortnight later.

BEA responded to BMA's all-year presence on the Jersey route by flying Viscounts from Manchester to Jersey via Birmingham on Mondays, Wednesdays and Fridays, after a fifteen-year break, from 1 November 1972. BMA much expanded its Jersey service in summer 1973 and also offered flights to the Isle of Man, Newquay and Guernsey.

On many occasions in the early seventies Elmdon was packed to bursting point with diverted aircraft, underlining its case for better facilities. This was particularly so before British Airways perfected its use of the Autoland system. On 4 January 1971 some 5,457 passengers were handled after fog had closed London's airports. The 1972/73 winter was little short of spectacular. On 20 December ten flights, mostly Tridents, diverted from Heathrow. On New Year's Eve a record forty-five flights diverted from Heathrow because of fog. The airport had to refuse further diversions because there was no place to park them. More diversions came in the following days. The apron and short runway were littered with Tridents, DC-9s, Boeing 707s, BAC One-Elevens, Viscounts and Vanguards. On 2 February ten flights, including a VC-10 and two Boeing 707s, diverted in; on 4th there were another thirty, including four VC-10s and three 707s. Despite a £106,000 extension to the old terminal building, on which work began in February 1972, it was becoming ever more apparent that dramatic action was needed. By July 1972 more than 5,000 passengers a day were being handled at weekends - more people than would use the airport in four months twenty years earlier. Industrial disputes - say, a strike by French air traffic controllers - would cause the lounges to overflow with passengers and their baggage in a matter of a few hours. The magic 'million in a year' figure for passengers came in 1973 - to be precise, on 19 October. On 30 October another thirty flights diverted from London and Manchester, with 2,091 passengers. These flights contributed £3,457 in landing fees, while the overtime bill incurred by the council for handling them came to just £40.

Although a common sight on IT work for some time, Dan-Air did not operate its first scheduled route through Birmingham until April 1972, when it commenced a service to Liverpool, Manchester and Bournemouth. Its service was cut from five to two flights a week, though, in April 1973. On 3 October 1973 Dan-Air operated its first scheduled Boeing 727 departure from the airport, when G-BAJW operated a charter to Tenerife.

From 1972 BEA, which had re-organised the previous autumn, based fifty cabin crew in Birmingham, twenty of them recruited locally. In 1973 three BAC One-Elevens were based at Elmdon, involving moving 120 pilots and crew, as well as engineers, to Birmingham. For the first time in twenty years British state airline aircraft and flying staff were based in the West Midlands, supported by the necessary service departments. The Viscounts on the Amsterdam service were replaced by Super One-Elevens on 2 April 1973 and those on the Dusseldorf weekday flights by Tridents. The fuel crisis at the end of the year cost ninety flights

Above: Central Air Services' Aztec G-AVRX, 17 July 1971. (S G Richards)

Right: The Airport Hotel before development. (Trefor Jones)

Below: Valetta VW197 arrived at Elmdon on 2 January 1969 for the Midland Air Scouts at Packington. It stood near the Coventry Road boundary while a strip was built at Packington for the aircraft to fly in. However, by the time the land had been prepared the Valetta had become unairworthy and it was broken up in November 1970. Only the nose section remained with the Scouts. (S G Richards)

Opposite: Prominent business operators have included: GKN's Islander G-AXXG; JCB's Dove G-ARJB both seen in 1971; C H Taylor & Co Ltd Cessna 414 G-AZFZ in December '74.

This page: A few military visitors: Queen's Flight Andover XS789 on 25 April 1972; Belgian Air Force Pembroke RM-5/OT-ZAE in May 1971; RAF Britannia C.Mk.1 XM489 'Denebola' on a trooping flight from Gutersloh on 24 October 1970. (all S G Richards)

and Viscounts were reinstated on some routes to save fuel. The London service was suspended from late 1973 to 29 April 1974, after which load factors on it were abysmal, falling from 65% to about 22%. The route now lost about £1,000 a day. Plans to open a service to Zurich were abandoned in February 1974. On the positive side, a third daily flight to Paris began in April and in November a new direct service opened to potentially oil-rich Aberdeen. We should not neglect to mention that by this time BEA and BOAC had fully amalgamated and become British Airways.

The East Midlands-based airline Alidair opened a scheduled service from East Midlands and Birmingham to Copenhagen using Viscounts on 30 April 1973. It planned to operate later to Milan, Zurich and Genoa. However, during 1974 British Midland asked to take over the Copenhagen route on the grounds that Alidair had not operated it since the beginning of the year. Alidair at first objected, blaming the oil crisis, but later withdrew. The Civil Aviation Authority awarded the route to BMA. Arrangements were made for BMA to open to Copenhagen in autumn 1977 but the day before the inaugural flight the Danish Government said the service was unacceptable and that landing rights would not be granted. The British Government retaliated against SAS and full-scale negotiations for a new Anglo-Danish Air Agreement began later.

The new airline Air Malta began weekly flights in 1974 using Boeing 720Bs wet-leased from Pakistan International Airways.

For ten years there had been lobbying by the controlling authority for a duty-free shop at Birmingham - the issue had even reached the attention of the Chancellor of the Exchequer. The Customs and Excise argued that too few foreign passengers used the airport to justify one, but they finally relented in January 1974.

On 11 November 1974 Air Anglia opened a Norwich - Birmingham service using Aztec G-AYTP, operated twice daily on Mondays, Wednesdays and Fridays. A Navajo Chieftain was introduced in November 1975. Between 1974 and 1978 it commenced services to Swansea and Newquay, followed in April 1979 by a twice-daily Chieftain service to Humberside. Air Anglia amalgamated with British Island Airways, BIA/Air West and Air Wales in January 1980, to form Air UK.

By 1975 British Airways was losing so much money on its route to London (71-seat Viscounts) that the future of the service was very much in question. Then, to the surprise of many, British Midland joined British Airways on the route, using the 50-seat Herald G-BAVX to operate three flights a day from 1 November 1975. BMA expected to get 50,000 passengers in its first year, but in July 1976 revealed that it had in fact carried 70,000 and was making good profits, thanks to lower overheads and more appropriate aircraft than the state airline. BMA added a fourth flight to Heathrow in September 1976 and by 1979 was carrying more than 100,000 passengers on the route. DC-9 jets were introduced by BMA to Brussels and Frankfurt in April 1978, cutting flight times to sixty and eighty minutes respectively.

The British Airways Paris route switched from Orly to the new Charles de Gaulle airport in spring 1976. From April 1978 British Airways operated a BAC One-Eleven service to Milan, on Mondays and Fridays.

On 4 June 1978 Elmdon received its first Boeing 747, when VH-EBH of Qantas visited.

KLM's short-haul subsidiary, NLM, opened a weekday F.27 Friendship morning service from Amsterdam. NLM's F.28 Fellowship jet PH-CHB was named *City of Birmingham* on 8 July 1979 by the Lord Mayor. To mark the International Year of the Child, eighty handicapped youngsters from the city were given a half-hour flight. Fellowships operated from April 1981, but the Friendship was restored in October. The Fellowship returned in April 1984.

Perhaps inspired by the success of the British Midland service to Heathrow, British Caledonian opened a twice-daily feeder service to Gatwick, using the seven-seat Piper Navajo Chieftain G-SCOT, later joined by G-CLAN. Capt Eric Rowley piloted the inaugural flight. Before long, though, British Caledonian found the route expensive to maintain and applied to the Civil Aviation Authority for Brymon Airways to be designated as a joint holder of the licence and take over operation of the route. This they did in October 1979, 20-seat Twin Otters giving a flight time of fifty-five minutes. The frequency was later increased to three services daily. An additional flight on Sundays was announced in July 1981.

The small Jersey-based airline Air Intra opened a thrice weekly Birmingham - Lyons Viscount service in November 1978. Prospects for the service were enhanced by the fact that the two cities are twinned, but after only two months it was abruptly withdrawn.

Opposite:
The Navajo Chieftain used by British Caledonian to open its Gatwick-Birmingham service. (BCAL)
NLM's Fokker F.28 PH-CHB was named 'City of Birmingham' on 8 July 1979. To mark this event, 80 handicapped youngsters were given a flight over the city. (Frank Ffitch, KLM)
Birmingham's first Jumbo, 1978. (Qantas)

The main development of 1978, though, was a remarkable deal between British Airways and British Midland. BA was losing £1½ million on its routes out of Liverpool and wanted to concentrate on serving nearby Manchester. BMA was keen to be the major presence at Liverpool but less enthusiastic about being the under-dog at Birmingham, which it felt it would always be. So BA exchanged its licences for four routes out of Liverpool and also that for Belfast - Isle of Man, in return for BMA's unused Birmingham - Copenhagen licence and its routes to Brussels and Frankfurt, which between them attracted 40,000 passengers a year. BA made Birmingham the headquarters of the sales area that embraced Wales and the South-West. Seven BAC One-Elevens were based in Birmingham, plus 100 pilots and ninety cabin crew.

British Airways carried 417,893 passengers on scheduled services to and from Birmingham, and about 650 tons of freight a month, in 1978. A weekday service to Milan began in 1978, followed by a service via Manchester to Copenhagen in April 1979. A route to Zurich via Brussels began in April 1980.

However, this new confidence in the commercial promise of the Midlands was ill-timed. The state airline was undeniably inefficient and the new Conservative government expected an early return to profitability. One of the first measures in the dramatic British Airways rationalisation programme was to dispense, at last, with the remaining Birmingham - London flight, on 1 April 1980. The direct service to Aberdeen ended the following October. The services to Jersey and Guernsey, the jewels in the state airline's crown at Birmingham twenty years before, also went. The Brussels/Zurich and Milan routes closed on 31 March 1982, followed on 26 March 1983 by the Copenhagen service. A Sunday service to Nice opened on 22 May 1983 but lasted only a few months.

Brymon's role in operating British Caledonian's service from Gatwick has already been mentioned. Brymon was first evident at Birmingham when it opened a service from Plymouth on 2 May 1979. This was twice daily on Mondays, Wednesdays and Fridays. In the summer of

Resident light aircraft - early 1970s:
Midland Aero Club Rallye G-AWJI
(Henri Ducommun)
Arthur Harrison's Aero 145 G-AROE on 31 March 1974. (S G Richards)
Piper Colt 108 G-ARON of the Warwickshire Aero Club on 7 April 1974. (S G Richards)
Warwickshire Aero Club's Reims Cessna F.152 G-OWAC, 16 September 1980. Air France's Concorde F-BTSC behind. (S G Richards)

1980 it was operated twice daily on weekdays and daily at weekends, but the following summer was only once daily and went via East Midlands. By the summer of 1983 the route had closed.

In May 1979 Dan-Air opened a twice-weekly service to the Isle of Man and added an extra flight to Newcastle.

A weekly summer service from Larnaca, operated by Boeing 707s, was opened by Cyprus Airways in 1981.

Hundreds of Irish punters fly into Birmingham each year for the Cheltenham Gold Cup. On 13 March 1979 Aer Lingus had ten flights scheduled in, but three were condensed into a load of 370 for a Boeing 747, which did two round trips from Dublin that day, carrying 400 on the second.

The first visit to Birmingham by Concorde was on 16 September 1980, when Air France's F-BTSC flew in from Charles de Gaulle Airport, Paris. A British Airways example came on 21 March 1982, in the shape of G-BOAE from Heathrow.

On 3 January 1982 Air-India opened a twice weekly Boeing 707 service from Bombay, via Delhi, Amritsar and Moscow, which has been well supported.

The last British Airways Viscount service, from Aberdeen via Manchester to Birmingham (commanded by Capt Bob Parker with sixty-seven passengers on board), operated on 26 March 1982.

British Midland recommenced the service to Brussels immediately after BA abandoned it and from 1 April 1982 operated it twice daily with F.27 Friendships. Up to five flights a day to Heathrow are also offered. Friendships operated until spring 1983, when the Shorts 360 G-BMAJ (joined in March 1984 by G-BMAR) took over.

In the spring of 1983 Birmingham Executive Airways was formed to operate smaller airliners on longer business routes that aircraft like the BAC One-Eleven could not operate profitably. It received its Air Operator's Certificate on 1 June. Operations started on 6 June with two 18-seat British Aerospace Jetstream 31s - G-CBEA *Spirit of Birmingham* and G-OBEA *Spirit of West Midlands*, both registered on 29 March - with a third on order. A service to Zurich, flown daily from Monday to Friday, opened on 8 June and one to Copenhagen, operated twice each weekday, commenced the next day. Since 6 June 1983 Birmingham Executive has also operated to Aberdeen on contract charter to British Airways. A third Jetstream 31, G-WMCC, *Spirit of Mercia*, was delivered on 3 October. A weekday service to Milan opened on 1 November; it would have been earlier but for a disagreement with Alitalia, which did not have a revenue sharing agreement with Birmingham Executive as it had previously with British Airways. An extra Sunday service to Copenhagen started on 5 February 1984. Routes to Geneva, Stuttgart and Stockholm are planned. A route to Geneva opened on 9 April and approval to operate to Stuttgart and Stockholm has been secured, subject to further capital being raised. A Grumman Gulfstream I is being purchased in the USA, and is expected to be named *Spirit of Enterprise.*

Also during summer 1983 Securicor's subsidiary Skyguard commenced a twice-daily parcels service to Belfast using Herald G-AYMG. On 26 September the Chieftain G-SAVE was delivered and a service to Brussels opened on 28 November. A route to Dublin is being planned.

Several organisations continue to offer club flying and tuition, including Birmingham Avia-

British Airways Concorde G-BOAA at the far end of the western apron. (British Airways)

tion with Aztec E G-BBHF, Cessna F.172M G-BGNR, Reims Cessna FRA.150M Aerobat G-CLUB, Reims Cessna FA.152 G-FLIC (formerly G-BILV) and Warrior G-BJCA (owned by John Duffin). The Warwickshire Aero Club flies Cessna F.152s G-OWAC and G-OWAK, both registered to the club on 11 July 1980. G-OWAK was damaged in July 1983 when it was blown over by the blast from a British Midland Boeing 707. Its Reims Cessna F.172M G-BDPH was damaged in a heavy landing in 1983. The Birmingham Aero Centre has Aztec F G-SHIP, which is for sale, Arrow IV G-WEND, which is owned by J Wyer, Cessna F.152s G-CPFC and G-BIDH (the latter owned by C Bluck), Arrow G-BCGD and Cherokee G-BCVV. Finally, Elmdon Aviation has Cessna 414A G-BTFH.

Nearly half of the passengers using Birmingham International Airport now use holiday charter flights. Horizon operates its own airline, Orion, whose first Boeing 737 flight from Birmingham was in March 1980. Intasun operated twenty-one flights a week out of Birmingham in summer 1983, thirteen of them by Air Europe, which based a Boeing 737 there. Britannia Airways Boeing 737s continue to be a familiar sight; in January 1984 they were operating to Monastir, Palma, Malaga, Alicante, Tenerife, Faro and Munich; Aviaco had DC-9s and Boeing 727s to Alicante, Malaga and Tenerife.

Prospects for summer 1984 include Wardair Boeing 747s operating to Toronto, Cyprus Airways A310 Airbus flights to Larnaca (as well as a weekly Boeing 707 between 15 July and 15 September) and visits by Iberia A300 Airbuses on charter to Aviaco. Air India hopes to introduce Boeing 767s in early 1985 and British Midland have long-term plans for a New York service.

The particularly severe impact of the recession on the West Midlands has, without doubt, affected traffic - particularly on scheduled services. However, traffic related to exhibitions at the NEC has grown steadily and has compensated to a significant degree. An easing of the recession, together with the opening of a Duty Free Zone and the promotion of Birmingham as a Convention Centre, could produce an unprecedented growth of traffic in the late 1980s. Fortunately, at last Birmingham has the terminal for the job.

Boarding British Airways One-Eleven G-BBMF 'County of Worcestershire', 1983. Most of the Birmingham-based fleet are named after Midlands counties. (British Airways)

Securicor's Dart Herald G-AYMG.

Aer Lingus One-Eleven EI-ANG, 21 July 1974.

Britannia Boeing 737 G-BAZI, winter 1979. (all S G Richards)

This page:
Tupolev Tu-134A YU-AHX of
the Yugoslav airline Aviogenex.

Ghana Airways VC-10 9G-ABO
diverts in, 2 January 1971.

Dan-Air's Boeing 727-46
G-BAEF escaping from snowy
Birmingham, 21 January 1978.

Summer season line-up on the
international apron, 13 June
1976. (all S G Richards)

Opposite page:
Four Orion Boeing Boeing 737s
on the international apron, 14
November 1981. The nearest
aircraft is G-BHVI, the 737th
737 built. (Orion Airways)

British Midland Boeing 707-338
G-BFLD, 4 December 1983.
The almost complete new
terminal can be seen.

British Airways Boeing 747-236
G-BDXJ arrives to be named
'City of Birmingham' by the
Lord Mayor, on 10 October
1980. (British Airways)

The Motor Show at the NEC
attracts large numbers of private
and corporate visitors, usually
being parked on the short
runway. (Airport Collection)

Towards '84

Between 1960 and 1967 the number of passengers using Birmingham Airport doubled, whilst the number of commercial aircraft movements rose by less than a tenth. The planners' predictions for future growth, especially once the main runway had been extended, made it clear that the airport could not cope for much longer simply by periodically tacking extensions on to the 1939 building. The original terminal was, anyway, beginning to look shabby. There was a growing appreciation, too, that airports ideally should be linked directly to motorways and railways.

The idea of a railway station adjacent to the airport was revived in 1966 by a councillor but promptly rejected by British Railways, on the grounds that it would encourage people to use the railways' principal source of competition.

A £2.8 million expansion plan, including a new terminal, to enable the airport to cope with two million passengers a year by 1980 was approved by the Airport Committee in June 1967 but rejected by the City Council. The Airport Committee submitted a fresh scheme for a terminal building in September 1969 - one on the south-west side of the terminal, towards the Coventry Road, costing £2 million. Again, the plan was still-born.

In August 1968 the Birmingham Chamber of Commerce suggested a National Exhibition Centre to an all-party Commons Committee. The Chamber proposed that the NEC should be on the site of the airport, and the airport itself moved to Honiley. Not surprisingly, Birmingham Council opposed the idea. In January 1969, though, the Chamber and the Council jointly recommended the site between the airport, the Birmingham-London railway and the A452 road. The Government also considered a site near Northolt aerodrome in Middlesex, but in January 1970 opted to back Birmingham.

The concept of a new airport terminal next to the NEC was first mooted in May 1970. Plans for a £3 million terminal were drawn up. On 22 February 1971 the Airport Committee voted unanimously for a new terminal costing £9.75 million.

The issue was given urgency by the Government's go-ahead for the NEC in November 1971. Two years later Michael Heseltine, the Aerospace and Shipping Minister, promised a decision on the airport terminal by February 1974. In December 1973, though, the Civil Aviation Authority recommended that the Government reject the scheme - now estimated to cost £11 million - as the traffic generated by the NEC would not represent more than 10% of the airport's business. By March 1974 the estimated cost had spiralled to £20 million and the oil crisis was creating havoc for forecasters of airline traffic.

Responsibility for the airport passed from Birmingham City Council to the new West Midlands County Council in April 1974.

Birmingham and Manchester were designated by the CAA in 1975 to be the major international airports for central England, with others, like East Midlands, Liverpool and Coventry on a less favoured footing. This resolved a long-standing debate as to whether Birmingham's old terminal should be extended and East Midlands Airport developed more vigorously, instead of building a completely new terminal at Birmingham. The CAA noted that the introduction of quieter jet aircraft by 1990 would minimise disturbance to local people at Elmdon. In 1978 a Government White Paper on national airport policy designated Birmingham as a category 'B' regional airport, meaning that it would concentrate on regional needs for international services rather than on inter-continental flights. Thus it should not - at least in theory - compete with Manchester.

The National Exhibition Centre opened at Bickenhill on 2 February 1976, alongside the new Birmingham International Railway Station.

In 1979 Peter Shore, Labour Secretary of State for the Environment, told West Midlands County Council to submit a planning application to him for a £29 million scheme, to included a new terminal near the NEC and a new aircraft taxiway. He said the basic issues were whether the development was in line with Government policy for the development of regional airports, and whether this was the right way to meet future traffic demands. Environmental questions were also to be considered. A public enquiry opened on 27 September 1979 and closed on 1 November.

The final, long-awaited go-ahead came on 29 May 1980. Construction work commenced on 10 April 1981. The contract was awarded to John Laing Construction Ltd, which quoted £40,599,929.09. This figure was subject to adjustment to take account of inflation. About £20 million is coming from a Government cash grant. The West Midlands County Council received the keys to the new terminal on 11 January 1984, twelve weeks ahead of schedule.

Before describing the new development, it is perhaps interesting to reflect on what might have been. Several options were considered before the present location and layout were agreed. One was to build a new passenger terminal on the A45 between the old building and Sheldon, at the southern end of the short runway, which would be closed. Car parking would have been on the south side of the A45. This option would have made Birmingham a one-runway airport and a bigger noise nuisance to people in Sheldon, whilst still not giving direct access to the railway and the NEC. Another option was to have the new terminal immediately next to the car parks at Birmingham International Station, with links to aircraft piers about 400 and 600 metres away.

The new Birmingham International Airport terminal has been designed to cope with three million passengers by 1990 and up to 33,000 aircraft movements annually. The terminal building is a three-storey steel frame structure, clad in moulded panels and tinted glass wall units. Two piers serve twenty aircraft stands (eleven international, of which five are for wide-body jets and nine domestic, three of which are for wide-bodies). The public areas in the building are dramatically bigger than in the old terminal, allowing a much more comprehensive provision of shops, travel and financial services, restaurants, buffets and bars. The duty-free shop is much bigger. There is an 800-space multi-storey car park immediately next to the terminal building (not a 200 yard stagger away, as at the old site) and open-air parking spaces for 4,400 vehicles.

All check-in desks are in the main hall on the ground floor, but the international departure lounges are on the first floor, segregated from domestic passengers at ground level. The third floor houses administrative offices.

On the roof is what promises to be a superb spectators' gallery, with a covered area and buffet, reached by lifts and stairs from the outside of the building.

Space for yet further expansion has carefully been left available.

One of the headaches for aircrew and air traffic control officers in the past has been that the main runway has doubled up as a taxiway. This has been remedied by the construction of a taxiway, parallel to the main runway on the Marston Green side. A 'lazy lane' is also provided for aircraft not requiring to use the whole length of the runway.

Below: The new Birmingham International Airport terminal, with its two aircraft piers. The elevated MAGLEV track linking the airport to Birmingham International station and the NEC can also be seen. At the bottom of the picture are the sides of the bridge that carried aircraft over the railway during the war.
(West Midlands County Council)

At the western end, there is a loop off the new taxiway big enough to take two jets, which will enable the order in which aircraft take-off to be changed at short notice. Effectively, the main runway itself has been slightly lengthend by the provision of 'run-on' tarmac at both ends. The construction of the new apron and taxiways used 130,000 cubic metres of crushed stone and 240,000 tons of concrete.

Residents of Marston Green are shielded from aircraft noise by two earth barriers, one of which is forty feet high and a mile long.

The airport's fire service has a long history of efficiency, the evidence of which is the large number of awards it has won over the years. Its job has not been made any easier, though, by the cramped accommodation it has had by the hangars. This has been remedied by the building of a new fire station, which is situated north of the main instrument runway and west of the short one, just off the eastern end of the new long taxiway. Time and tyre rubber will be saved by the facility to drive through the station, and not to have to reverse vehicles in.

Easily the most novel feature of the new terminal, though, is the £4 million MAGLEV shuttle link between it and Birmingham International Station. Running on a 620 metre

Above: A MAGLEV car under test. This £4 million shuttle link between the new airport terminal and Birmingham International station has not been without its teething troubles, but hopefully it will prove to be an efficient and popular system and a valuable 'shop window' for British technology.

Below: View of the new terminal from under the MAGLEV elevated track.

elevated track, driverless carriages 'float', by means of magnetic levitation, half an inch over a track. It has a linear electric motor. Each carriage weighs five tons and carries up to forty people and their luggage. Each journey takes ninety seconds and the frequency will be at least every two minutes.

MAGLEV has been developed by the People Mover Group, a consortium including four GEC companies, Balfour Beatty Power Construction, Brush Electrical Machines and Metro-Cammell. The cars were built at Washwood Heath by Metro-Cammell. The first was delivered on 21 March 1983. The project was financed by West Midlands County Council, British Rail and the private sector. British Rail (Research and Development) were technical advisers.

Linear motors have long been used in industry to power factory production lines, to work heavy doors and drive parts of cranes. However, this is the first time the linear motor's potential for transporting people has been properly exploited. It was a deliberate decision by the airport authorities not to use the Westinghouse system, as at Gatwick, because it was more expensive than MAGLEV and not British.

The development of MAGLEV has not been troublefree - but then, genuine technological innovation rarely is. Assuming that it works efficiently, MAGLEV could be a valuable 'shop window' for a developing aspect of British applied science.

As though to crown the endeavours of those responsible for the new terminal, the Government announced on 2 February 1984 that Birmingham International Airport is to be one of six sites in the UK where freeports will be developed. The freeport, or Duty Free Zone, could create 1,000 new jobs on airport land next to the Coventry Road. It will offer industry the opportunity to make, store and process goods in a zone that is free of customs control. Duties, such as advanced VAT payments, are incurred only when the merchandise leaves the Zone.

Birmingham's application was made on 28 October 1983 by West Midlands Freeport Ltd (WMFL), supported by West Midlands County Council, Solihull Metropolitan Borough Council and the Birmingham Chamber of Industry and Commerce. The first phase will involve the development of six hectares on the Birmingham side of the Excelsior Hotel, providing 17,700 square metres of units and a 6,300 square metre Cargo Transit Building. It is anticipated that 'high value/low weight' products, such as jewellery and electronics, will be prominent there. It is hoped it will be operational by the early summer of 1985.

The first official departure from the new terminal was on 22 March when BAC One-Eleven G-BGKG of British Airways, chartered by West Midlands County Council, left for a day trip to Bordeaux. Operations were switched from the old terminal to the new site on 4 April 1984. The first departure from the new terminal that morning was by Birmingham Executive's Jetstream 31 G-OBEA to Zurich and Geneva: the aircraft was piloted by Captain Dennis Holmes with first officer Tony Hubbard. Unfortunately British Midland's first departure, a Friendship bound for Brussels was delayed for three hours after its nosewheel tyre punctured as the aircraft taxied to the runway.

Her Majesty the Queen and His Royal Highness the Duke of Edinburgh will officially open the new complex on 30 May. This will be preceded by public open days over the Bank Holiday weekend of 26-28 May, when many aircraft, including Concorde, are expected to be shown.

The new terminal will undoubtedly stimulate air transport in the Midlands and consequently create desperately needed jobs. It is pleasing that Vic Turton, who was so energetic in the 1960s in preaching the virtues of having a modern airport in the West Midlands, should be Chairman of the County Council in the year the new terminal opens. The present Airport Committee Chairman, Councillor Colin Beardwood, has staunchly defended the decision to have MAGLEV and played a key role in getting the freeport. Bob Taylor MBE, the Airport Director, has been involved with the project for virtually a decade and commands the admiration and affection of the entire airport community. A car accident in 1976 made Bob the only airport director we know 'with his own undercarriage', but it is testimony to his guts and professionalism that this fact is rarely even noticed by his colleagues. Asked recently to describe Bob Taylor, Capt Rod Clarke, Midlands Sales Manager of British Airways said, 'a bloody good airport director'. We concur.

Bob recently said to us that he hoped that the wide expanses of the new terminal would not distance employees from each other and that the airport would continue to be known as a friendly one. This is one risk that must be avoided, and the other is to allow complacency. Nothing has ever come to Birmingham Airport without the most persistent lobbying and campaigning. Pressure on Whitehall must be maintained, and if the Government carries out its intention to abolish the West Midlands County Council, an effective airport management structure that involves the whole region must be speedily devised.

The people of the West Midlands should see the airport as one of their most valuable investments - and one that will only pay good dividends if they themselves use it to the full.

113

The new terminal seen in full operation on Monday 9 April; British Midland's latest aircraft Shorts 360 G-BMAR in use on the Heathrow service.

A British Airways One-Eleven on one of the new air bridges. Birmingham Executive's Jetstream 31 G-OBEA. Passenger terminal exterior. The new passenger concourse. (all photos Geoffrey Negus)

Around and About

Air Training Corps aircraft

The Air Training Corps has had many units in and around the city, cultivating an aviation interest amongst the younger generation. Some of the most visible signs of their presence have been the various aircraft issued to them for training and/or exhibition purposes. Amongst these have been:

Blackburn B.2 G-ADFU. To 1415 Squadron, King Edward's Grammar School, Birmingham 2.42, allocated 2903M. Struck off charge as scrap 28.5.47 and removed by the RAF.

D.H.60X Moth G-EBTH Donated to a unit at Sheldon in 1940; burnt 1950/51.

Fairchild 24-C8C G-AECO. Impressed as BK869, allocated 3129M for 1347 (Elmdon) Squadron at Olton, delivered 15.6.42.

Supermarine Spitfire XII MB855. 5379M for 487 Squadron, Kingstanding. An enquiry from the unit as to how to prolong the life of the aircraft resulted in a visit from 71 MU who chopped off the wings and removed the aircraft - no date known.

D.H.82A Tiger Moth N6720. 7014M issued to 481 Squadron, West Bromwich 18.3.53; transferred to 493 Squadron, Haunch Lane, Kings Heath 12.4.77.

DHC.1 Chipmunk T.10 WB758. 7729M ex-Gaydon Station Flight, with 2030 Squadron, Barrows Lane, 3.68 but returned to 71 MU 9.67, thence to Torbay Aircraft Museum.

Hawker Hunter F.4 XF941. 8006M ex 229 OCU. Delivered to 2030 Squadron, Barrows Lane 3.68; transferred to Hawker Siddeley Aviation at Baginton in 1972.

A.W. Meteor TT.20 WD646. 8189M ex 3 CAACU delivered late 1972 to 2030 Squadron, Barrows Lane; still present recently repainted in camouflage with 84 Squadron markings.

Hawker Hunter WB195. 7284M. Ex-Hawkers (for whom flown by Neville Duke) and Henlow, stood in the grounds of Solihull Grammar School from 1960 and sold for scrap 1967.

Bristol Sycamore 3 G-ALST/WA577. 7718M for 492 Squadron, Haslucks Green Road, Shirley, delivered 20.6.72. Moved to 493 Squadron, Haunch Lane in 1978, but was passed to the North East Aircraft Museum, Sunderland in 1980.

D.H. Vampire T.11 WZ450. With 2371 Squadron at Wilfred Martineau Upper School, Tile Cross; said to have arrived 12.74 from Royal Air Force Association, Wrexham.

D.H. Vampire T.11 XD377. 8203M. With 487 (Kingstanding) Squadron at Perry Barr, delivered 7.72 from 27 MU.

D.H. Vampire T.11 XD602. 7737M. Delivered to 494 Squadron at Smethwick, but due to vandalism transferred to 495 Squadron at Sutton Coldfield 1.70.

E.E. Canberra WT534. Nose section only delivered to 489 Squadron 29.3.82.

The Scout A.H.1 helicopter XT625 is gate guardian at St George's Barracks, Rectory Lane, Sutton Coldfield. It arrived in June 1979, was first painted incorrectly as XR625, now XR777.

In September 1942 Air Training Corps cadets of 476 Squadron at Vickers-Armstrong, Castle Bromwich, started construction of a Cadet glider. Various components were constructed by 495 Squadron (Sutton Coldfield), 165 Squadron (Fort Dunlop) and 482 Squadron (Wolseley). Work on a second aircraft commenced in 1943. The first glider took to the air on 16 July 1944 and officially handed over to Air Marshal Sir Leslie Gossage on 29 July, when it was flown by Gp Capt J A Cecil Wright MP, Midland Aero Commandant of the ATC (and former 605 Squadron commander) at Castle Bromwich.

Below: Hunter WB195/7284M at Solihull Grammar School. (Roy Bonser)

Local Exhibitions
Various service recruiting and promotional displays have been staged from time to time in parks and other suitable open spaces in the city. Examples include:

Summerfield Park - mid-September 1967.
An RAF exhibition, mostly consisting of static display aircraft from 71MU: Gnat XM693, Javelin 7975M, Hurricane PZ617 'AF-T', Sedbergh WB983, Spitfire K9942. Hunter XF946, Sycamore HC.14 XG540, Hunter nose XE643, a Lightning nose, Shackleton nose WG511 and a Vulcan nose.

Billesley Common
Used on several occasions, the earliest known to us being July 1947 when a V-1 'Flying Bomb', A-4 (V-2), Ohka (Japanese piloted missile) and Rheintochter (German ground-to-air guided missile) were shown.
An Army display on 25 and 26 July 1970 included the 'Blue Eagles' display team of Sioux helicopters (XT134, XT206, XT511, XT193 and XW192), with MQM-57 Drone XT581 on the ground. A much larger RAF exhibition was held from 11 to 27 August 1972 with flypasts and demonstrations on most days.

Cannon Hill Park
The 'International Spring Festival' held here

Above: Spitfire I K9942 on display at Summerfield Park in September 1967. This aircraft is now in the custody of the Royal Air Force Museum at Hendon. (S G Richards)

has often included RAF and Royal Navy static display aircraft, and, at least in 1970 and 1971, balloon races.

Civic Centre, Broad Street
An exhibition of militaria captured during the war was held in September 1945 next to the Civic Centre, at the city end of Broad Street. It included a V-1 'Flying Bomb' and the Heinkel He162 jet 120095.
During June 1946 a Navy League Exhibition was held here, featuring Firebrand EK745, Firefly PP600, Seafire 17 SX278 and a Swordfish. The RAF exhibited here in August 1946. The show included Tempest Mk.V NV758, Typhoon Mk.1B SW659, Vampire TG315 and Spitfire Mk.XIV RM729.

Birmingham Museum of Science and Technology, Newhall Street
Displayed here are Hurricane Mk.IV KX829 and Spitfire Mk.LF.IX ML427, and also the cockpit section of a Beaufighter I.

Helipads

Helicopters are of course versatile enough to land in any suitable open space, and often do so. Royal visits have often brought Queen's Flight Wessex helicopters to various city parks and RAF 'Rescue' Whirlwinds and Wessex have made ambulance flights to hospital sports grounds. Industrial concerns have also used helicopters to visit factories, building sites and so on, and of course the BBC studios at Pebble Mill Road, Edgbaston, have often been visited by helicopters and VTOL aircraft. Apart from the Hay Mills heliport of the early 1950s, there have been two other 'formal' heliports: Fort Dunlop, used by various helicopters in the early 1970s, but now closed; Moor Hall Hotel at Sutton Coldfield. The National Exhibition Centre has had a field set aside as a helipad and on occasions during exhibitions it has been quite well used. Solihull Metropolitan Borough Council is considering opening a helipad near the town centre.

Below: Sea Harrier FRS.1 XZ451 of 700A Squadron, Yeovilton, landing on the BBC Social Club's football pitch behind the Pebble Mill studios, 20 September 1979. (S G Richards)

Scrap Metal Merchants

Several scrap metal dealers have taken aircraft scrap from time to time, and although most is quickly processed, some substantial hulks of aircraft have been known to linger for years in such yards. There are two major yards locally:

BKL Alloys, Kings Norton
Most fairly quickly torched, but noted in March 1959 were various Meteors and Attackers. In March 1969 parts of Javelin XA544 and various Vulcans, all of which came from St Athan, were seen. Later in 1969 there were parts of Buccaneer XK491, Meteor WB174 and Beverley XM103.

Minworth Metals Ltd, near Castle Bromwich
A yard thought to have been most active during the 1950s and early 1960s, when dozens of aircraft of many types were dealt with - for instance, in February 1960 several Meteors of various marks were present, along with two Hunters, many Venoms, Expeditor HD775 and Sikorsky Hoverflys KN841, '842 and '862. The former British European Airways Junkers Ju52/3m G-AHBP, which had been stored at Elmdon, was brought here by 7 July 1948 and the fuselage used as a tea-room by the workers. Also known to have come here is the fuselage of Prentice G-APIF from Croydon when that airport closed.

Dunton, near Curdworth

605 Squadron records mention a 503 Squadron Fawn crashing at Dunton Hall Forward Landing Ground on 4 March 1928. There were no casualties but the aircraft was written off. We assume that this was at the private strip owned by Bill Breedon, which one of our informants said was active in about 1931. Alan Cobham's circus called here on Saturday/Sunday 9/10 June 1935. Klemm L-25-I G-AAXK was kept here whilst owned by John Wynn in 1939; Wynn was interned in the war for his fascist sympathies, and the Klemm was damaged by damp while it was stored in his absence. G-AAXK was damaged when a hangar collapsed at White Waltham in March 1962 and is thought to be at Sevenoaks now, being restored. Wolseley based Tomtit G-ABOD at Dunton in the 1930s for engine testing. J Hassall kept his Comper Swift G-ABPR here in 1938, and possibly in nearby Coleshill during the war. Drone G-AEJS, Moths G-AAFI, G-AAKI and allegedly G-AARI were also here before the war. The site was made unusable by the erection of high-tension pylons nearby.

Below: Don Burgoyne's Dicer 'G-AECN' at Honiley. (Walter Wincott)

Above: Comper Swift G-ABPR, a pre-war resident of Dunton, visiting Castle Bromwich. (M Butler)

Knowle

Don C Burgoyne of Chadwick Manor, Knowle, built with H Stirling a low-wing monoplane called the Burgoyne Stirling Dicer, unofficially given the registration G-AECN. Although constructed in 1939, it did not fly until the project was resurrected at Honiley in 1946. The Dicer is thought to have been a conversion of BAC Drone G-AEDB, which Burgoyne bought in late 1938, to a tailskid aircraft, utilising parts of the crashed Drone G-AEEN and the engine of Dart Pup G-AELR, which had crashed at Tachbrook Aerodrome, Leamington. It is reported to have made four short hops at Hockley Heath on 31 March 1946 and accumulated about four hours' flying during April and May. Another report says it flew at Syerston in Nottinghamshire. Burgoyne sold the Dicer to Percy Nadin of Stoke-on-Trent, but it was bought back by Burgoyne who stored it for a number of years. Eventually it was sold to someone in Workington.

Burgoyne also owned several other light aircraft. They included the original and legitimate G-AECN, a Pou du Ciel, which according to one report never flew, but according to another flew at Bushwood (four miles south of Knowle) on 9 February 1936. It was used by children as a pony trap and its registration was cancelled in November 1945. During the war Burgoyne repaired gliders for the Air Training Corps. Sometime during the war he owned Klemm L.26 Mk.IIIA G-ABOJ.

Until 1949 Burgoyne owned the British Klemm Swallow G-ACXE (the aircraft that ten years before had been the second to land at Elmdon). Drone G-AEJH was dismantled at Heronfield, Knowle, in September 1948; the energetic Mr Burgoyne almost certainly had a hand in this. In 1953 the Drone G-AEJR was reported to still be at Chadwick Manor.

D.H.60 Moth G-EBLV was kept in a field at Knowle from August 1938 by its owner, J F Jefferson. It crashed at Castle Bromwich on 5 February 1939, was sold to the makers and later restored.

Marston Green

A Vickers aircraft, possibly a Venture, crashed at Marston Green on 25 November 1927 and was salvaged on 27th. Alan Cobham's circus visited a site in Bickenhill Lane on Saturday 3 August 1935. Admission was 1s-3d, flights were from 3s-6d. Lt Owen Cathcart-Jone's Monospar was featured. Bickenhill Lane runs between the National Exhibition Centre and the new airport terminal, so it is not completely beyond the bounds of possibility that Cobham and his colleagues were the first people to fly from the site of what is now Birmingham International Airport.

Below: Fred Taylor and his B.102 aircraft. (Science Museum, London)

Solihull

Alan Cobham's circus stopped at Widney Road on Sunday 17 June 1935.

J G Wood built Mignet Pou du Ciel G-AEBT at Solihull between 4 August 1935 and 15 May 1936. It may have incorporated parts bought from Mr Ackers in March 1936 for £7 - Ackers had started building a Pou in late 1935 but gave up the following year. G-AEBT was registered to Wood and C Smith-Vaughan and first flew on 1 June 1936. Tested at Walsall, its last flight was only eighteen days later. In 1937 it was owned solely by Wood. It was stored until 6 May 1946, when it was sold to J A Fortney. It was seen at Fortneys Garage, Corporation Street on 16 June 1948. The Birmingham Branch of Air-Britain acquired it in June 1951 and stored it at a house in Middleton Hall Road, King's Norton. The father of the Air-Britain member evicted it (shame!) a year or more later. It was last heard of at the 'Treasure Trove' junk shop, Cotteridge, in October 1952.

Sutton Coldfield

R C Streather built Pou G-AEOH in late 1936. It stopped flying in 1938 - at the request of Mrs Streather! The fuselage was used as a motorcycle side-car. The remains were purchased by Bob Ogden of Solihull in 1967, who built a new fuselage. It was later sold to Gordon Riley.

The Taylor Ultra-Lights

Birmingham bricklayer Fred Taylor designed and built, with Len Bracey, a series of ultra-light aircraft in the 1930s and 1940s. Their serials had no official significance. They all had the letter 'T' (for Taylor?) on the tail. First was A.101, a single seat open-frame aircraft. Then B.102, a single-seat high-wing monoplane powered by a pusher engine. This survived the war and flew in the late 1940s. C.103 was called the Wagtail. Built at a cost of £15 in Taylor's council house bedroom, it flew from a farm, possibly at Marston Green. It was a single-seat parasol monoplane powered by a JAP J-99. Becuase it was built with unapproved materials, it could not be registered. It was stored during the war and later fitted with a Bristol Cherub sold to them by Don Burgoyne of Knowle. It flew to Castle Bromwich on 2 October 1948, then Elmdon, where it was charged 12s-6d, although an illegal aircraft!. It is said later to have been sold to Arthur Harrison and later to Councillor Bevin. The fourth Taylor aircraft was D.104, a two-seat trainer based on the C.103. Taylor emigrated to Australia in 1950, built another ultra-light there and even attempted man-powered flight.

Aircraft Production During First World War

AUSTIN
R.E.7
Contracts A2860, A2940 and A2733 issued in 1915. 33 ordered, includings nos 2237-2266 (30 aircraft), of which 2241, 2242 and 2260 went to Royal Naval Air Service and remainder to Royal Flying Corps.
R.E.8
100 aircraft ordered under contract 87/A/488 in August 1916. 150 aircraft ordered under contract 87/A/785 in September 1916. 300 aircraft built, serials A3169-3268, A4261-4410 and B5851-5900.
S.E.5a
Contract A.S.22251 for aircraft B8231-8580. Contract A.S.9141 for aircraft C7901-8550 but order cancelled in favour of A.S.22251 and serials re-allocated. Contract A.S.22251 for aircraft C8661-9310, of which C8738, '40, '43, '45-47, '49-50, '52-54, C9076-78, 9080-86 and 9088-90 went to United States Air Service. Contract 35a/387/C.280 for aircraft E5637-5936. Contract 35a/1764/C.1883 for aircraft F7951-8200, of which F7951-8200 went to United States Air Service. Contract 35a/1764/C.1883 for aircraft H5291-5540 cancelled before aircraft built. From B8485, delivered in about March 1918, Austin's 251st S.E.5a, the wooden 3-strut undercarriage replaced the weaker V-struts type.
Bristol F.2B
600 ordered, to be H5940-6539. But only H6055 and H6058 confirmed delivered.

BIRMINGHAM & MIDLANDS CARRIAGE CO
Handley Page O/400
D5401-5450 and F301-320. Another batch, J2242-2291, was planned but deliveries up to J2275 only are known to heave been completed. Nine aircraft from this batch were later civilianised.
De Havilland D.H.10
Within the serial range E6037-6136.

METROPOLITAN CARRIAGE, WAGON & FINANCE CO
Handley Page O/400
D4561-4660 (100 aircraft) built. A further 75, to have been K3542-3616, ordered but cancelled.
Vickers F.B.27 Vimy
E9737-9856 (100 aircraft) ordered but cancelled.

WOLSELEY MOTORS LTD
B.E.2c and B.E.2e
Nos 2470-2569
B.E.2e
A3049-A3148
S.E.5a
C6351-6500 (order no A.S.11452); D6851-7000 (order no A.S.30281); F851-950 (order no 35a/534/C.410); F7751-7800 (order no 35a/1756/C.1865. Wolseley built the engine for early S.E.5a A4868 (no.627/2233/W.D.8202) and 35 of the second batch of S.E.5as had Wolseley-built 150hp Hispano-Suiza engines. Later 200hp Hispano-Suizas were used - with difficulty, although 700 were ordered. Delivery of the 200hp engines began in March 1917. In the event 449, designated the W.4b Adder, were delivered, all but four of them in 1917. In later S.E.5a production, it is believed that 100 Python and 4,250 Viper engines were used. Steel tube V-struts were used on earlier S.E.5as but as these did not stand up well to operational use Wolseley changed to wooden 3-strut undercarriages from its 151st aircraft (presumably D6851).

Sopwith T.F.2 Salamander
Contract (no.35a/1674/C1777) for 150 aircraft, to have been F7601-7750, cancelled.

Austin Whippet Production
Aircraft listed in order of Constructors Number:
A.U.1 K-158. Registered to Austin 14.7.19. Became G-EAGS. CofA issued 4.12.19. Owned by Austin - not sold. Withdrawn from use with CofA expiry on 19.11.21. Marks lapsed.
A.U.2 G-EAPF. Registered 11.19. CofA issued 7.10.24 or 17.7.24. Sold to FOSoden, then possibly others, but after August 1925. Delivered by air to Midland Aero Club, Castle Bromwich by Soden 15.7.26. Rarely used. Made forced landing with no damage 26.9.26. Bought by club member E R King in summer 1928 to fly to Blackpool Air Pageant, 6-7 July, but he sold it soon after, possibly to Herbert M Pearson at Hamble in 4.29 without the CofA, which expired 27.4.29. This Whippet was reported to be all-silver with black letters. Faded into disuse by 11.32.
A.U.3 G-EAUZ. Registered 7.20. CofA 30.7.20. Sold to A J Greenshields, who shipped it to Argentina in 10.20 where it was re-registered R-151. Still flying there in 1928.
A.U.4 Imported into New Zealand early 1921 by R A Dexter, Auckland. First flown 27.5.21. Sold to H H Shaw, Hamilton 30.5.21. Reported to have been the first privately-owned aircraft in New Zealand and first to make Auckland-Hamilton flight. To P Coleman, Wanganui, who registered it ZK-ACR 1.5.31. To W R Bennett, Taihape 7.8.31. Crashed at Kai Iwi, near Wanganui 1932. Inspected 1935 and withdrawn from use. Registration cancelled 12.11.37. Fate unknown.
A.U.5 Imported into New Zealand by R A Dexter 1921. Never flown. After storage sold before 1924 to a circus as a prop. Believed taken overseas.

Civil Aircraft Based at Castle Bromwich
The Midland Aero Club (MAC) was active at both Castle Bromwich and Wolverhampton in the 1930s but it is doubtful whether aircraft were confined to either airfield, so all MAC aircraft, including those registered at Wolverhampton, are listed.

G-EAFQ Avro 504K. Telford J Rogers. Based from August 1919 until September 1921.
G-EAHH D.H.6. Warwick Aviation. CofA 13.8.19.
G-EAHI D.H.6. Warwick Aviation Co. Curtiss OX-5 engine. CofA 7.8.19.
G-EAHU Avro 504K. W L Woodward. Based from 5.22 until it crashed at Castle Bromwich on 10.6.22.
G-EALE Avro 504K. Midland Aviation Co from 8.22. CofA renewed 9.22. Cancelled 24.4.23.
G-EAPF Austin Whippet - see Appendix B above.
G-EAVU/Y/Z Sopwith Pups presented by James Palethorpe, a Club Vice-President, to MAC when it opened at Castle Bromwich 6.10.25.
G-EBLT D.H.60 Moth. MAC, received under Air Ministry subsidy scheme, 8.25. To makers in part exchange for Moth Major, 1934. MAC fleet no 1.
G-EBLW D.H.60 Moth. Received by MAC under Air Ministry subsidy scheme, delivered 25.9.25. MAC fleet no 2. Crashed at Shirley 3.11.29.

G-EBQX D.H.60 Moth. Registered to D L Lloyd and G F M Wright 31.10.32. Registered to D L Lloyd only 2.3.35. Registered to H S Griffiths, Walsall 31.1.36. Registered to E J Brighton, c/o Airviews, Castle Bromwich 20.10.36. Stored after C of A expiry 6.10.37 and moved to Gatwick November 1939.

G-EBST D.H.60 Cirrus Moth. Critchley Grahame, based from December 1933 to April 1935.

G-EBTH D.H.60 Cirrus Moth. Based from about 1928 by David Kittel, who kept it in a hangar near the Toro Soap Works. Registered to Harold J Willis 23.3.31. Registered to P H I Jones, Elmdon 24.7.39.

G-EBTI D.H.60X Moth. Registered to S P Jackson in December 1929. Sold December 1930.

G-EBTO S.E.5a. Walter L Handley (owned garage in Suffolk Street). Based from January 1929 until withdrawn from use in December 1929.

G-EBXT D.H.60X Moth. MAC. Presented either by Wolverhampton Express & Star or by a local firm J B & N D Graham. 'Wulfrun', MAC fleet no 3. Delivered in 1928, converted to D.H.60G. Stored from 1936 to August 1937, when sold.

G-AABH D.H.60X Moth. MAC (fleet no 5), bought March 1930. Sold November 1934.

G-AADB D.H.60X Moth. MAC (fleet no 4). Based from late 1928. Sold April 1935.

G-AAEZ Avro 504K. Aeroplane Services Ltd. Based from March 1929, probably until 1933.

G-AAFI D.H.60G Gipsy Moth. S P Jackson, from 1931. Sold before 1935.

G-AAJJ D.H.60G Gipsy Moth. MAC, early 1930s. Sold February 1934.

G-AAKD D.H.60G Gipsy Moth. Bought by Arnold Methley 7.29 and registered to him 9.29. Sold to C W R Gleeson, Castle Bromwich (and County Clare, Ireland) 1930. Sold March 1934.

G-AALT D.H.60G Gipsy Moth. Capt Walter L Handley Based January to April 1934.

G-AANB Desoutter 1. Eric C Fairbairn. Based from July 1935 until moved to Elmdon September 1939.

G-AAPK Desoutter 1. F P Smith. Based 7.35 - 8.36.

G-AASI Hawker Tomtit. Wolseley Motors Ltd. Based from July 1933. Used to test fly the Wolseley A.R.9 Mk.1a, and in 1935 the Wolseley Aries. Sold 4.36.

G-AAWR D.H.60 Moth. Eric J Brighton, registered in May 1930. Possibly also owned or used by Major C M Pickthorne in June 1930. Sold to Midland Air Services Ltd 1931. No valid C of A 6.4.35 - 18.2.37, but sold in December 1937.

G-AAZH Klemm K.25C. Leslie A Willard. Based in 1939. Moved to Whitley.

G-AAZP D.H.80A Puss Moth. Horace G Everitt. Based for short period before moving to Elmdon 9.39.

G-ABAX Hawker Tomtit. Wolseley Motors Ltd. Based from May 1933. Fitted with geared A.R.9 Mk.1a radial and flown in 1933 King's Cup Race. Sold 9.36.

G-ABDR D.H.60 Moth. Charles E Hewitt, registered 25.7.30. Crashed (on roof of house?) at Erdington on 12.7.31. Hewitt killed; passenger Baker (a Flying Officer with 605 Squadron) seriously injured.

G-ABIA D.H.80A Puss Moth. R Hope. In September 1941 housed at Henry Hope & Sons Ltd, Smethwick. To T C Sparrow 1.4.41. Impressed 31.5.41.

G-ABOD Hawker Tomtit. Wolseley Motors Ltd. Based from May 1933. Fitted with direct drive A.R.9 Mk.IIA and flown in King's Cup Race. In 1938, fitted with a Wolseley Aquarius, became personal mount of Hawker test pilot W Humble.

G-ABYU D.H.80A Puss Moth. H L Johnson. Based in 1935. Left on European tour to include Cologne, Milan, Berne and Brussels 27.5.35. W H Sutcliffe co-pilot.

G-ABZK D.H.Moth Major. MAC, from April 1938. Assumed moved to Elmdon 6.39. Scrapped 11.45.

G-ACAC Bristol 96 Fighter. W L Handley. Based from

April 1933. Scrapped at Hooton January 1936.

G-ACHU Monospar.

G-ACJF General Aircraft Monospar ST-4 Mk.II. G S Davidson. Based from 12.34. Withdrawn from use 4.39.

G-ACNR D.H.Moth Major. MAC. Bought via Brian Lewis & Co May 1934 (fleet no 10). Sold May 1940.

G-ACOG D.H.Moth Major. MAC. Bought via Brian Lewis & Co May 1934 (fleet no 7). Sold August 1940.

G-ACOH D.H.Moth Major. MAC. Bought via Brian Lewis & Co May 1934. Lost in fatal air collision with Hart K3887 of 605 Squadron over Castle Bromwich 9.12.34.

G-ACOI D.H.Moth Major. MAC. Bought via Brian Lewis & Co May 1934. Equipped for blind flying, returned to Club April 1934. Sold August 1940.

G-ACTW D.H.Moth Major. MAC. Bought September 1934. 'Returned after being completely rebuilt' - *Contact* magazine, 15.8.35.

G-ACVI Airspeed Envoy. Lord Nuffield. Named 'Miss Wolseley'. Equipped with Wolseley III radial engines. Was to have flown in Mildenhall - Melbourne race, but damaged previous evening. Flew to Portugal and back early 1935. Based from October 1934 to August 1936.

G-ACWA Klemm L.25C. E or V L Parry. Based from August 1934. Sold to H L Johnson May 1939. Moved to Coventry 31.8.39.

G-ACXE See 1939 Elmdon list in Appendix E, p.123.

G-ADAP D.H.95 Leopard Moth. Alfred Ellison FRGS from April 1935. Alfred and John Ellison flew to Morocco, reaching Casablanca 20.4.35. Toured Morocco for six days. Won Coupe Compte de Montigny and came second in Fedallah Race. Returned to Castle Bromwich 27.4.35. Reported late 1935 that Ellisons were about to depart for Tripoli. Later in summer visited Balkans. In October to Kenya where aircraft sold, becoming VP-KBU.

G-ADDI D.H.84 Dragon II. Vickers-Armstrong Ltd. Bought 15.7.43.

G-ADMF BA Swallow 2. Based from July 1935. Owned by H E Hudson until sold to J K N Evans in December 1938 (but Evans flew it to Ringway 3.7.38). Based until June 1946.

G-AEDX BA Swallow 2. P R Burton and V M Desmond (who joined MAC June 1934). Based 3.36 to 5.39.

G-AEKK Miles M.3B Falcon. Dunlop Rubber Co Ltd. Based July 1936 to January 1940.

G-AELG BA Swallow 2. A H Wallis, from 12.9.42. Later with B Smith.

G-AEOA D.H.80A Puss Moth. On 1.9.39 with owner W H Leadbetter, at 386 College Road, Erdington. Impressed 31.5.41, owner notified 9.6.41.

G-AEOE D.H.82 Tiger Moth. MAC. C of A valid 12.36. To W S Shackleton Ltd and sold abroad 25.6.40.

G-AEXH BA Swallow 2. E E Hughes-Williams. Based April 1937 until March 1939.

G-AFAV Percival Vega Gull. Air Hire Ltd, circa 1937-1939.

G-AFCN Miles M.11A Whitney Straight. H M Mitchell. Based October 1938 to April 1939.

G-AFIB Hawker Tomtit. Alex Henshaw. Based from 2.41. To Vickers-Armstrong Ltd 8.41. Used as road block, October 1943.

G-AFIW Percival Q.6. J Brockhouse Ltd.

G-AFJB Foster Wikner Wicko. MAC. Bought November 1938. Sold July 1940. Now preserved at Berkswell.

G-AFNP/R/S/T/U/V D.H.82A Tiger Moth. MAC. C of A effective 3.2.39.

G-AFTA Hawker Tomtit. Alex Henshaw. Based 6.42 to 2.46. Now preserved by Shuttleworth Trust.

G-AFVV Hawker Tomtit. Alex Henshaw. Based from February 1941. Cancelled November 1945.

G-AGEF Hawker Tomtit. Vickers-Armstrong Ltd. Written-off when collided on take-off with parked Spitfire, pilot Henshaw, 18.10.43.

605 Squadron Aircraft at Castle Bromwich

Unless otherwise stated, aircraft survived their stint with 605 Squadron and were passed on to other units. Aircraft marked with an asterisk were new when taken on strength. The pre-war squadron code was HE.

D.H.9A E8656, E8686 (first squadron aircraft; dual control; delivered 25.10.26), E8711 (del from Henlow 23.5.27), J7814 (arrived by air from Henlow 1.11.26), J8107 (damaged in collision 8.28), J8109 (erected and engined by by Auxiliary AF personnel, air-tested on 9.10.27), J8125 (reserve aircraft, del by air 14.8.28), J8162 (collected from Brooklands 16.4.29), J8163, J8208 (del from Eastchurch 3.2.28), J8225 (del by air from Henlow 5.1.28), J8480 (dual control aircraft, del from Westlands by air 22.4.27). Squadron records also mention a D.H.9A '7184' which force landed and crashed (P/O Edwards) on exercise, 16.8.28, but this aircraft cannot be traced.

D.H.60M Moth K1206 (force-landed in bad weather and written-off 19.1.35), K1216 (with squadron from 26.4.34 to 25.1.35).

Avro 504K E9543 (del 7.1.27), E or H3017 (del by air from Henlow 20.1.27), E or H3068 (del by air from Henlow 2.11.26, allotted to Halton 24.3.27), F9828 (arrived from Henlow by air 26.10.26, to Halton on 21.4.27), H2402 (del by air from Henlow 13.1.27), J738 (del 21.12.26, fouled telegraph wires on take-off and crashed, P/O Knox VC unhurt, 9.4.27).

Avro 504N J8510 (arrived from Manchester 28.3.27), J8511 (arrived from Manchester 30.3.27), J8686 (undercarriage collapsed while taxying, Castle Bromwich 9.1.30), J8689 (del 3.4.28), J8711 (crashed on take-off and burst into flames, pilot badly burnt 4.8.29), J8772 (collected from Henlow 27.5.27), K1806, K1968, K1987*, K2364*, K2387*.

Wapiti IIA J9651, J9837 (crashed in heavy landing at Castle Bromwich 25.3.34, possibly repaired), J9864 (known to be squadron's 7th Wapiti, del 12.4.30), J9865, J9866, J9868, K1146*, K1147, K1148*, K1156* (struck off charge 10.7.34), K1157*, K1342, K1343*, K1367, K1368, K1370* (converted to Wallace K4016 2.33), K1376* (struck off charge 23.10.34), K1377* (struck off charge 17.5.34), K2237* (Mk.VI dual control aircraft, del 1931), K2238* (del 1931).

Hawker Hart K1423, K2435, K2452, K2458, K2459, K2461, K2465, K2467, K2989, K3010, K3017, K3018, K3032, K3051* (del 1933), K3756* (first Hart with 605, assembled by unit, first used for dual instruction 27.10.34), K3861, K3877, K3883* (del 1934), K3885* (del 1934), K3886* (del 1934), K3887 (del 1934, collided with Moth G-ACOH and crashed near Castle Bromwich 9.12.34), K3888* (del 1934), K3889* (del 1934), K3890* (del 1934), K3891* (del 1934), K3892* (del 1934).

Avro Tutor K3309 (believed went with 605 to Tangmere), K3311, K3457* (undershot in forced landing 2 miles from Castle Bromwich 2.7.39), K3458*, K3459* (crashed in forced landing 24.6.37).

Hawker Hind K5431, K5467, K5531* (del 1936), K5532* (del 1936), K5533* (del 1936), K5534* (del 1936), K5535* (del 1936), K5537* (del 1936), K5538* (del 1936), K5539* (del 1936), K5540* (del 1936), K5541* (del 1936), K6672, K6674, K6676, K6726, L7237*.

Gloster Gladiator I K6145, K7917, K7942 (coded HE:H), K7946 (coded HE:R), K7952, K7961, K7965, K7979, K7985, K8004, K8032, K8044.

Gloster Gladiator II N2303*, N2304*, N2305*, N2306*, N2308*, N2309*, N2310*, N2311*, N2312*, N2314*, N5576* (del 3.39), N5577*, N5578*, N5580*, N5581*, N5583*, N5585*, N5586* (coded HE:K).

Fairey Battle N2108, N2109.

Hawker Hurricane I L2012*, L2013*, L2014*, L2018*, L2020*, L2121.

Aircraft not known On 7 January 1928 a 605 Squadron aircraft crashed in Tarnham Park, with pilot Flg Off Bohlero and passenger Flg Off Wykes. On 2 September 1928 P/O Aldridge, on a cross-country flight from Henlow to Castle Bromwich via Waddington, crashed on the second leg at Great Glen, Leicester, and was killed. The aircraft burst into flames on impact. On 28 July 1929 Flg Off Nock, possibly in a D.H.9A, flew into a hedge at Wormleighton, Warwick, after the engine cut.

Elmdon Based Aircraft 1939

G-EBTH D.H.60X Moth. Philip H I Jones. Based from July 1939 until presented to Air Training Corps 1940.

G-AANB Desoutter I. Eric C Fairbairn. Moved in from Castle Bromwich 9.39. Sold in November 1939.

G-AAYW Avro 625 Avian. Capt W L Handley. Registered in his name 23.8.39. Scrapped 1940.

G-AAZP D.H.80A Puss Moth. Horace C Everitt of Knowle. Believed moved from Castle Bromwich to Elmdon 9.39. Impresssed into military service 9.41.

G-ACXE Klemm Swallow. Birmingham Garages Ltd (Councillor Goodby). Later impressed but still on civil register in 1946.

G-ADJX D.H.87A Hornet Moth. Thomas Carlyle. Moved to Walsall by 20 December.

G-ADKS D.H.87B Hornet Moth. V M Desmond Impressed 7.6.40.

G-ADKV D.H.87B Hornet Moth. E E H Williams. Impressed 2.3.40.

Austin Production 1938-45

Fairey Battle
L4935-5797 (863 aircraft, delivered October 1938 - August 1940). R3922-3971, R3990-4019, R4035-4054 (100 aircraft, delivered October 1939 - May 1940. Believed delivered in knocked-down state, majority to Royal Canadian Air Force and remainder to Australia and South Africa). V1202-1280 (66 aircraft, delivered August - October 1940). V1281-1594 (serials of 234 cancelled aircraft). Austin also received K7587 when it was new, presumably as a production pattern aircraft. It passed it to the Royal Aircraft Establishment. It also retained L5522 before passing it to the RAF. Battle R3950 has been preserved.

Hawker Hurricane IIB
AP516-550, AP564-613, AP629-648, AP670-714, AP732-781, AP801-825, AP849-898, AP937-956 (300 aircraft).

Short Stirling Mk.I
191 aircraft, ordered under contract 982939/39. Delivery dates in brackets: W7426-7475 (December 1940 - February 1942); W7500-7539 (February - May 1942); W7560-7589 (May - July 1942); W7610-7639 (July - September 1942); BK592-628 (September 1942 - March 1943); BK644-647 (December 1942 - February 1943).

Short Stirling Mk.III
429 aircraft. Delivery dates in brackets: BK648-667 (December 1942 - February 1943); BK686-727 (January - June 1943); BK759-784 (March - May 1943); BK798-818 (April - June 1943); EH875-909 (May - July 1943); EH921-961 (June - September 1943); EH977-996 (August - October 1943); EJ104-127 (September - November 1943); LK375-411 (September 1944 - January 1945); LK425-466 (November 1943 - February 1944); LK479-521 (January - March 1944); LK589-624 (May - October 1944). BK660 crashed during a test-flight on 10 January 1943. It stalled at 1,000 feet and nose dived into a field off the Coventry Road near Elmdon. The crew was safe.

Avro Lancaster
100 Mk.B.I aircraft, delivered March 1944 - February 1945: NN694-726, NN739-786, NN798-816. Up to NN806 these aircraft had Merlin 22 engines; thereafter Merlin 24s. 50 aircraft ordered March 1943 as Mk.B.I with Merlin 24 engines, delivered as Mk.VII interim aircraft February - November 1945: NX611-648, NX661-703, NX770-794. 30 Mk.B.VII aircraft of an order for 68, delivered November - December 1945: RT670-699. The following RAF serials were allocated for Lancasters to be built by Austin but cancelled: RT700-701, RT713-750, RT758-799, TG813-856, TG870-908, TG921-945. Austin-made Lancaster NX611, was preserved at RAF Scampton but to move to East Kirkby in 1984. NX662 is preserved at Perth, Australia, and a composite aircraft, NX665 with major components of NX666, survives in New Zealand.

Airspeed A.S.51 Horsa 1
300 fuselages for DP714-726, DP739-777, DP794-841, HG736-770, HG784-819, HG831-880, HG897-944, HG959-989.

Airspeed A.S.58 Horsa 2
65 fuselages for LF886-923, LF937-963.

APPENDIX G

Known 14EFTS Aircraft

Hawker Hind Operated early in the School's life. L7224, L7225.
de Havilland Tiger Moth K4251, K4254 (with School 15.10.39 - 1.8.40), K4260, K4283 (crashed in forced landing ½ mile west of Ansty 12.11.39), L6926, L6929, L6938, L6941, N5467 (crashed in forced-landing, Meriden 20.8.45), N5454, N5483, N5485 (hit cables in bad visibility, Elford, Staffs 13.7.44), N5488, N5489, N5490, N5491, N5493, N6445, N6446, N6447 (hit high-tension cables while flying low near Tamworth 1.1.40), N6449 'N', N6546, N6547, N6549, N6550, N6551, N6552, N6735, N6752, N6778, N6835, N6836 (crashed on take-off from Elmdon 10.7.45), N6854, N6862 (crashed in forced landing, Churton Heath, Warwick 6.12.45), N6868, N6920 (crashed in snow storm, Tamworth 20.1.45), N9115 (delivered 7.39, stalled and crashed, Maxstoke, Warks 10.12.40), N9145 (crashed in forced landing, Halesowen 1.3.45), N9154 (crashed on take-off, Elmdon 24.6.43), N9155 (crashed on landing, Nether Whitacre, Warks 10.5.44), N9156 (hit balloon cable and abandoned near Castle Bromwich 8.11.41), N9158 (spun into ground 2 miles NW of Elmdon 9.1.42), N9176, N9184, N9186, N9192, N9194, N9212, N9214, N9238, N9239, N9240, N9252 (with School 22.4.41 - 21.8.42), N9336 (crashed in forced landing, Northfield 19.6.44), N9518 (two spells with School), N9521, R4773, R4774, R4782, R4845, R4848, R4851, R4875, R4907, R4949, R4956, R4967, R5023, R5024, R5025, R5026, R5027 (side-slipped

into ground, Nether Whitacre, Warks, 3.4.44), R5029, R5030, R5060, R5112, R5178 (stalled at low altitude, Knowle LG, 24.4.41), R5216, T5607, T5595, T5628, T5843 (with School 20.7.40 - 25.7.45), T5844, T5845, T5846 (hit high-tension cable low flying 2 miles W of Kingsbury 15.5.41), T5847, T5848, T6047 (hit blister hangar on approach,Hockley Heath 22.5.45), T6048, T6049 (crashed in practice forced landing, Nether Whitacre, Warks 17.3.44), T6122, T6123, T6124 (hit hangar on over-shoot, Elmdon 19.6.44), T6125, T6238, T6571 (blown over while taxying, Elmdon 3.1.45), T6910 (collided with T5982 of 7 EFTS and crashed, Elmdon 11.5.45), T6990, T7027, T7088, T7095, T7108, T7153, T7210, T7211, T7216 (hit tree in forced landing near Aldridge 7.2.41), T7217, T7222 (stalled during low aerobatics, Allesley 19.7.45), T7229, T7234, T7236, T7237, T7238, T7240 (crashed on take-off, Elmdon 10.12.43), T7241, T7285, T7368, T7393, T7473, T7609, T7678 (crashed in forced landing, Nether Whitacre 5.7.45), T7840, T8002, T8258, T8263, T8264 (hit high-tension cable recovering from a dive, Kingsbury 1.7.41).

APPENDIX H

Spitfire Production at Castle Bromwich

The Mark numbers are those of the aircraft when first flown. In January 1940 Castle Bromwich received the fuselage of Spitfire I N3296 for use as a pattern aircraft and N3298 and '9, which actually were sets of parts.

1,000 Mk.IIA aircraft, ordered 12 April 1938. First aircraft delivered 27 June 1940: P7280-7329, 7350-7389, 7420-7449, 7490-7509, 7520-7569, 7590-7629, 7661-7699, 7730-7759, 7770-7789, 7810-7859, 7880-7929, 7960-7999, 8010-8049, 8070-8099, 8130-8149, 8160-8209, 8230-8279, 8310-8349, 8360-8399, 8420-8449, 8460-8479, 8500-8531, 8533-8536, 8540-8541, 8543-8549, 8561-8563, 8565-8577, 8579-8580, 8582-8584, 8586-8599, 8601-8602, 8605, 8608, 8641-8679, 8690-8698, 8701-8702, 8704-8706, 8725-8729. These 921 aircraft built as Mk.IIA/IIB. Remaining 79 built as Mk.VA/VB: P8532, 8537-8539, 8542, 8560-8561, 8564, 8578, 8581, 8585, 8600, 8603-8604, 8606-8607, 8609, 8640, 8699-8700, 8703, 8707-8724, 8740-8759, 8780-8799. The last aircraft, P8799, delivered 21 July 1941.

500 Mk.I ordered 22 June 1940, but changed to Mk.V. Delivered 25 July 1941 (AB780) to 23 November 1941 (AD583 and '4): AB779-828, 841-975, 892-941, 960-994, AD111-140, 176-210, 225-274, 288-332, 348-397, 411-430, 449-478, 517, 535-584.

1,000 Mk.III ordered 24 October 1940. Delivered as Mk.VB between 23 November 1941 (BL231) and 16 May 1942 (BM653): BL231-267, 285-304, 311-356, 365-391, 403-450, 461-500, 509-551, 562-600, 613-647, 655-699, 707-736, 748-789, 801-833, 846-864, 887-909, 918-941, 956-998, BM113-162, 176-211, 227-274, 289-329, 343-386, 399-430, 447-493, 508-543, 556-597, 624-653.

905 Mk.VC ordered 23 August 1941, delivered between 6 April 1942 (EN763) and 4 September 1942 (ER199): EN763-800, 821-867, 887-932, 944-981, EP107-152, 164-213, 226-260, 275-316, 327-366, 380-417, 431-473, 485-523, 536-579, 594-624, 636-669, 682-729, 747-795, 812-847, 869-886, 888-915, 951-990, ER114-146, 159-200.

750 Mk.IV delivered between 29 August 1942 (ER206) and 20 December 1942 (ES368): ER206-229, 245-283, 299-345, 461-510, 524-571, 583-626, 634-679, 695-744, 758-791, 804-834, 846-894, 913-948, 960-998, ES105-154, 168-214, 227-264, 276-318, 335-369. All completed as Mk.VB/VC.

989 Mk.VB ordered 1 January 1942, of which 976 were Mk.VB/C and 13 Mk.IX: JG713-752, 769-810, 835-852, 864-899, 912-960, JK101-145, 159-195, 214-236, 249-285, 303-346, 359-408, 425-472, 506-551, 600-620, 637-678, 705-742, 756-796, 803-842, 860-892, 922-950, 967-992, JL104-140, 159-188, 208-256, 301-338, 346-395.

1 F.21 originally ordered from South Marston, changed to Castle Bromwich 24 April 1944: LA187. (Alex Henshaw says in Sigh for a Merlin that he flew this aircraft from South Marston on 27 January 1944).

680 Mk.VC ordered 28 February 1942. Delivered as 300 Mk.V and 380 Mk.IX (some were converted to Mk.IX off the production line). Delivered between 28 March 1943 (LZ807 and '8) and 1 June 1943 (MA906): LZ807-848, 861-899, 915-956, 969-998, MA221-266, 279-315, 328-369, 383-428, 443-487, 501-546, 559-601, 615-657, 670-713, 726-767, 790-819, 831-863, 877-906.

2,190 Mk.V/IX ordered 28 May 1942. Delivered between 1 July 1943 (MH298) and 29 April 1944 (ML427): MH298-336, 349-390, 413-456, 470-512, 526-568, 581-626, 635-678, 691-738, 750-800, 813-856, 869-912, 924-958, 970-999, MJ114-156, 169-203, 215-258, 271-314, 328-369, 382-428, 441-485, 498-536, 549-589, 602-646, 659-698, 712-756, 769-801, 814-858, 870-913, 926-967, 979-999, MK112-158, 171-213, 226-268, 280-326, 339-379, 392-428, 440-486, 499-534, 547-590, 602-646, 659-699, 713-756, 769-812, 826-868, 881-926, 939-967, 981-999, ML112-156, 169-216, 229-277, 291-323, 339-381, 396-428. All were Mk.IX except MH298-311, 564-568, 581-596, 600, 605, 637-646 (46 aircraft).

600 Mk.IX ordered 1 December 1942, but first 232 cancelled (123 on 15 August 1945 and 109 on 15 November 1945). Remaining 368 aircraft built as Mk.IX and delivered between 28 April 1944 (NH148) and 14 June 1944 (NH611): NH148-158, 171-218, 230-276, 289-326, 339-381, 393-438, 450-496, 513-558, 570-611.

800 LF.IX ordered 2 June 1943 but contract altered many times. 282 aircraft completed as F.22s: PK312-356, 369-412, 426-435, 481-525, 539-582, 594-635, 648-677, 680, 715.

1,500 F.21 (Victor) ordered on 6 June 1943 from Castle Bromwich and South Marston. Order altered many times. In the end, 14 Seafire F.47 PS944-957 completed, plus 688 F.IX and 5 LF.XVI at Castle Bromwich. First, PT335, delivered 28 June 1944: PT335-380, 395-436, 451-498, 523-567, 582-627, 639-683, 697-738, 752-795, 818-859, 873-915, 929-970, 986-999, PV115-160, 174-215, 229-270, 283-327, 341-359.

100 LF.IX ordered on 25 October 1943. Delivered between 18 August 1944 (RK799) and 11 October 1944 (RK925). 35 went to Russia; 25 were LF.XVI: RK798-819, 835-868, 883-926.

73 HF.IX ordered on 16 November 1943. 50 built as Mk.IX, remainder as LF.XVI. Delivered between 17 August 1944 (RR181) and 18 October 1944 (RR264): RR181-213, 226-265. RR233 collided with SM212 at Castle Bromwich on 19.10.44 and was not rebuilt.

1,500 F.21 ordered 21 January 1944 but only 197 Mk.IX and 366 LF.XVI built. Delivered between June and August 1945: Mk.IX: SL594-595, 625-635, 648-665, SM135-150, 170-177, 240, 425, 441-463, 486, 504-506, 508-510, 513-515, 517-537, 539-548, 563-597, 610-645, 647, 663, 666, 668-669. LF.XVI: RW344-359, 373-396, SL541-565, 567-571, 573-579, 596-602, 604-605, 608-611, 613-618, 620-624, 666, 668-676, 678-681, 685, 687-690, 713, 715, 717-721, 724-727, 727-728, 733, 745, SM178-213, 226-239, 241-258, 273-316, 329-369, 383-424, 426-427, 464-485, 487-488, 503, 507, 511-512, 516, 538, 646, 648, 664-665, 667, 670-671.

1,884 LF.IX ordered 19 April 1944. Delivered between 29 November 1944 (TA739) and 23 June 1945 (TE578). 632 Mk.XVI and 850 Mk.IX (600 of which went to Russia) built: TA738-780, 793-840, 854-888, 905-948, 960-999, TB115-150, 168-197, 213-256, 269-308, 326-349, 352-396, 413-450, 464-503, 515-549, 563-598, 613-659, 674-718, 733-759, 771-808, 824-868, 883-925, 938-959, 971-999, TD113-158, 175-213, 229-267, 280-325, 338-379, 395-408, 952-958, 970-999, TE115-158, 174-215, 228-259, 273-315, 328-359, 375-408, 434-480, 493-535, 549-578. On 25 July 1944 199 HF.IX and 77 LF.IX were cancelled. All except one HF.IX were cancelled on 30 October 1944, and that aircraft cancelled in August 1945. On 6 March 1945 210 LX.XVI and 50 LF.IX were ordered; all were cancelled (as F.22s) on 18 August 1945. 54 incomplete fuselages were built and moved to South Marston where finished as F.24s. The rest of the order was cancelled. 135 F.24s were ordered in late 1945, amended to Seafire F.46/F.47 but later cancelled.

Many Spitfires were paid for by public subscription. The following were paid for by citizens of Birmingham: P7910, P7911, P7912 and P7913, named 'City of Birmingham' I to IV respectively. W3137 was named either 'BRUM 1' or 'BRUM 28' or 'BRUM 38'.

APPENDIX I

Lancaster Production at Castle Bromwich

HK535-579, 593-628, 644-664, 679-710, 728-773, 787-806, PP663-695, 714-758, 772-792. Up to HK773 aircraft had Merlin 22 engines; later ones had Merlin 24s. PP series aircraft delivered in 1945. 299 aircraft were actually made at Castle Bromwich but by agreement with Avro twelve aircraft were assembled in the flight shed. The first, DV272, was test-flown by Alex Henshaw on 16 October 1943.

APPENDIX J

Known 7AACU Aircraft

Airspeed Oxford N6268, N6294, N6296 (dived into sea on approach to North Coates 13.5.43), P1814, R6390 (hit trees and bridge during attempted forced landing on Coventry·Nuneaton road 28.2.43), V3532, V3604, V3872 (to 577 Squadron), V3873 (to 577 Squadron), V3877 (to 577 Squadron), V3880, V3884, V3886 (to Gosport, returned, later to 577 Squadron), V4025.

Bristol Blenheim IV V5500, V5623.

De Havilland D.H.90 Dragonfly X9337, X9389, X9390. All joined 3 May 1940; last left in August 1941.

Fairey Battle: L5011, L5034, L5047, L5205.

G.A. Monospar ST-25 Universal X9330, X9331, X9333, X9334, X9335. The first joined in April 1940. All except X9335 left in January 1941. X9335 crashed while taking off from Castle Bromwich 5.8.40, when engine failure forced the pilot to land in an obstructed field, where it hit a bank of earth.

Miles Master T8323, T8339, T8348, T8350, T8371, T8382, T8458, T8487, T8575, T8603, T8616, T8632, T8674, T8737, T8755, T8781. In Unit at least until April 1943.

Percival P.3 Gull Six X9391. With Unit December 1940 until November 1941.

Spartan Cruiser X9431, X9432, X9433. All arrived in May 1940; the last left in August 1941.

Westland Lysander L4752, L4755, L4767, L4781, L4788 (crashed in forced landing, Seven Lanes Farm, Castle Bromwich 21.11.40), V9293, V9311, V9373, V9426, V9433 (pilot overcome by fumes, Knighton 29.1.42), V9482, V9503, V9580 (hit ground in practice attack, Shrivenham 10.12.41), V9612 (hit balloon cables and crashed, Erdington 12.10.41), V9665, V9671, V9672, V9681, V9704, V9720.

APPENDIX K

Known 577 Squadron Aircraft

Squadron code: 3Y
Hawker Hurricane IIC/IV Type used December 1943 - July 1945. KZ325.
Vultee Vengeance Type used July 1945 - June 1946. HB 428 (Mk.IV)
Bristol Beaufighter Type used November 1944 - July 1945. LX957 (coded 3Y-J), NE716 (3Y:F), R2199 (Mk.IF), RD713 (3Y:R), T4640, V8353 (Mk.1F, struck off charge 8.7.46).
Supermarine Spitfire Mk.VB used June - July 1945, Mk.XVI June 1945 - 1946. Mk.LF.XVIE also used. AD111, BM569 (coded 3Y:F), SM199 (3Y:B), SM291, SM417 (3Y:Z), SM511 (3Y:J).
Airspeed Oxford Used throughout squadron life. N1194 (struck off charge 2.12.44), N6340, P1814 (ex 7 AACU), P1878 (ex 6 AACU), P1923 (ex 6 AACU), T1041, V3151 (coded 3Y:N, struck off charge 2.12.44), V3468 (ex 6 AACU, struck off charge 1.11.44), V3865 (ex 6 AACU), V3872 (ex 7 AACU), V3873 (ex 7 AACU, crashed in forced landing near Liverpool on 18.10.44), V3876 (ex 6 AACU, struck off charge 2.12.44), V3877 (ex 7 AACU), V3886 (ex 7 AACU, SOC 11.11.44), V4046 (ex 6 AACU, struck off charge 18.9.44), V4265 (hit buildings taxying at Wrexham 28.5.44).
Miles Martinet Type also used.

APPENDIX L

RAF Station Aircraft

Aircraft used by the authorities running the airfield and often loaned to resident units.

Castle Bromwich D.H.Tiger Moth: N9154, N9155, N9156, N9157, N9158, N9212, N9214, N9238, N9239, N9336. All except N9157 went on to Elmdon. Miles Master 1: T8575 (ex 7 AACU). Alex Henshaw in *Sigh for a Merlin* refers to a Dragon based by the RAF at Castle Bromwich.
Elmdon Gloster Gladiator I: K8052. Hawker Audax I: K3683, K3687.

126

APPENDIX M

Patrick-Duval Aviation and Patrick Aviation Aircraft

G-AGXC Auster J/1 Autocrat. Registered in December 1947, sold June 1950.
G-AGYF Auster J/1 Autocrat. Bought in 1947.
G-AHGH D.H.89A Dragon Rapide. Bought in June 1948, sold June 1953.
G-AHGI D.H.89A Dragon Rapide. Bought in June 1948, sold November 1952.
G-AHGS Percival Proctor V. Bought 12.47, sold 3.51.
G-AHTE Percival Proctor V. Bought 12.47, sold 6.48.
G-AHTG Percival Proctor V. Bought 12.46, sold 6.48.
G-AHTH Percival Proctor V. Bought in December 1946 crashed at Redditch on 8.3.48.
G-AIBB D.H.89A Dragon Rapide. Used 12.48 to 1.51.
G-AIOT Airspeed Consul. Named 'County of Warwick' Used January 1947 to December 1948.
G-AIOV Airspeed Consul. Named 'County of Worcester'. Used February 1947 to December 1948.
G-AJFF Miles Messenger 2A. Used 5.47 to 11.47.
G-AJFG Miles Messenger 2A
G-AJKP Miles Aerovan 4. Named 'County of Stafford' Used April 1947 to June 1952.
G-AJOF Miles Aerovan 4. Named 'County of Derby'. Used June 1947 to June 1952. Sold to E C (Ted) Cathels of Moseley, who as C & M Air Charters, flew it on freight and furniture removal charters. On 16 September 1950 it flew in the *Daily Express* Hurn to Herne Bay race but force-landed at Eastbourne. Sold to Chanair Ltd, Jersey in June 1952.
G-AJOI Miles Aerovan 4. Registered to Patrick Motors Ltd. Used from October 1950 until destroyed on the ground by a gale at Elmdon on 7.12.50.
G-AJZJ Miles Gemini IA. Bought in 1947.
G-AKDA Miles Gemini IA. Used 8.47 to 11.50.
G-AKHV Miles Gemini IA. Bought 1947/48 . . .
G-AKNX D.H.89A Dragon Rapide. Used 1.49 to 8.50.
G-AKNY D.H.89A Dragon Rapide. Used 1.49 to 1951.
G-AKOA D.H.89A Dragon Rapide. Used from January 1949 until the airline closed.
G-AKVU D.H.89A Dragon Rapide. Used 9.49 to 3.52.
G-ALRW D.H.89A Dragon Rapide. Used from December 1952 until the airline closed.

APPENDIX N

Aircraft of 5 Reserve Flying School

Squadron code: RCY

Avro Anson MG689, NK165, VV297, VV303 (R-40), VV309, VV310 (R-42), VV880 (RCY:V, later R-43, delivered 4.49), WB454.
D.H.82A Tiger Moth BB796, DE145 (R-14), DE211, DE364, DE526 (R-21), DE735 (believed crashed at Castle Bromwich 1948-50), DE784 (RCY:E), DE840 (RCY:F, with '6' on nose), DE978, DE982, DF211, EM735 (R-12), EM816 (R-17), N2955, N5476, N6552, N6624 (Spun into ground, Castle Bromwich 29.7.50), N6648 (?), N6848, N6946, N9255 (coded RCY:B), N9394, R5023, R5113, R5130 (with Unit 28.10.47 to 20.11.47), T5616, T5821, T6037, T6159, T6297, T6868, T6942, T7609, T7798 (RCY:H), W5014 (RCY-A).
D.H. Chipmunk WB665 (to BUAS, returned), WB667 (del 25.7.50, used by BUAS, coded U-11 and later C,

left unit 19.8.53), WB668, WB670, WB671, WB673 (R-27), WB675, WB676 (RCY:L), WB677, WB680 (del 17.6.50, left unit 21.5.53), WB681, WB682 (R-16), WB683, WB686 (R-29), WB687, WB706, WB715 (del 10.7.50, to BUAS 31.1.52, returned 30.11.52, left 24.7.53), WB716 (to BUAS, returned), WB717, WB718, WB719, WB720, WB721, WD385 (coded R-22, Z), WG307 (coded R-16, N), WG324, WG467 (R-15, hit trees during practice forced landing 1m NNE of Tamworth 24.9.53), WG480 (to BUAS), WG483 (to BUAS), WK523 (controls jammed during aerobatics, abandoned and crashed into bungalows, Sutton Coldfield 19.8.53), WK550 (to BUAS), WP779 (coded A, hit ground during low roll, Castle Bromwich 27.5.54, killing Flt Lt J Netherwood and a Birkett mechanic, D S Jones), WP784 (coded E), WP786 (coded B), WP789, WP790, WP791, WP793 (coded D, with unit 18.6.53 to 19.6.54), WP809 (R-27), WP829 (R-29), WP834 (to BUAS), WP835.
Percival Prentice VS362, VS366, VS381 (del 28.2.49), VS638 (del 30.9.49).

APPENDIX O

Birmingham University Air Squadron Aircraft (Pre-1958)

Squadron codes: RUB and FLK.

D.H.82A Tiger Moth DE364 (crashed on landing, Castle Bromwich 5.11.48), DE735 ('E'), DE842 ('B'), DE985, N6552 ('D'), NL910, NL985 ('A'), R4759, T6101, T6159, T7395, T7609 ('C'; to 5 RFS), T7840 (ex 14 EFTS).
Percival Prentice T.1 VS358, VS377, VS637, VS746 (del 16.6.50, struck off charge 17.7.57).
Avro Anson T.21 VV311, VV333.
N.A. Harvard FT227 and FX252 were 'loaned' by Helliwells for summer camp at Bassingbourn, 16-29 July 1950.
D.H. Chipmunk WB550, WB555, WB573, WB648 (with BUAS 1952, coded U-10, later 'A'), WB665 (5 RFS a/c), WB667 (5 RFS a/c, coded U-11, later 'C'), WB715 (ex 5 RFS, del 31.1.52, coded U-13, later 'E'; returned to 5 RFS 30.11.52), WB716 (5 RFS a/c, coded U-14, later 'B'), WB738, WD289 (for two periods), WD292, WD303, WD322, WD331, WD353, WD355, WD365, WG301, WG303, WG362, WG419, WG469, WG473, WG479 (for two periods), WG480 (ex 5 RFS), WG481, WG483 (ex 5 RFS), WG488, WK550 (ex 5 RFS), WK574, WK575, WK576, WK609, WP797, WP834 (visited Elmdon 15.2.58), WP839, WP843, WP851, WP854, WP862, WP900 (visited Elmdon 15.2.58), WP922 (visited Elmdon 15.2.58), WP970, WZ868.

APPENDIX P

Birmingham Airport: Movements

Year	Commercial	Non-Commercial	Total
1949	2,900	17,053	19,953
1950	4,182	9,667	13,849
1951	4,018	8,375	12,393
1952	4,208	10,137	14,345
1953	5,642	15,162	20,804
1954	6,321	9,094	15,415
1955	6,951	5,145	12,096
1956	9,627	12,342	21,969
1957	10,898	21,736	32,634
1958	9,710	15,172	24,882
1959	9,174	22,857	31,761
1960	13,779	17,407	31,186
1961	13,402	21,654	35,056
1962	12,845	19,143	31,988
1963	13,311	21,608	34,919
1964	14,264	25,944	40,208
1965	14,287	33,672	47,959
1966	14,345	31,388	45,733
1967	15,089	36,615	51,704
1968	15,287	39,081	54,368
1969	14,330	32,240	46,570
1970	14,344	31,984	46,328
1971	15,978	42,291	58,269
1972	19,068	43,279	62,347
1973	21,586	43,690	65,276
1974	20,397	39,188	59,585
1975	19,971	42,472	62,443
1976	21,936	44,374	66,310
1977	21,800	44,284	66,084
1978	27,741	43,214	70,955
1979	32,267	38,302	70,569
1980	31,731	49,791	81,522
1981	29,260	32,652	61,912
1982	30,102	33,548	63,650
1983	32,082	32,218	64,300

APPENDIX Q

Birmingham Airport: Traffic

Year	Total Passengers	Freight (Metric Tonnes)
1949	18,237	97
1950	31,440	185
1951	38,660	385
1952	46,489	213
1953	65,890	316
1954	90,163	482
1955	108,666	557
1956	154,806	622
1957	182,919	679
1958	168,893	770
1959	189,065	1,101
1960	283,833	2,295
1961	329,862	1,876
1962	348,319	1,866
1963	386,419	2,013
1964	431,806	2,385
1965	469,511	2,725
1966	534,558	4,159
1967	564,418	4,310
1968	572,172	4,976
1969	630,735	5,080
1970	702,559	5,543
1971	855,485	4,846
1972	969,718	4,308
1973	1,181,687	3,509
1974	1,056,002	3,116
1975	1,130,040	2,725
1976	1,157,635	2,648
1977	1,113,745	3,235
1978	1,352,978	3,201
1979	1,609,246	3,439
1980	1,604,015	2,921
1981	1,536,323	2,617
1982	1,611,066	2,211
1983	1,613,636	3,257

Bibliography

Andrews, C F and Morgan, E B: *Supermarine Aircraft since 1914*, Putnam: London 1981.

Andrews, P W F and Brunner, Elizabeth: *The Life of Lord Nuffield*, Blackwell: 1955.

Austin Motor Co: *How Longbridge Spanned the Years of War - Austin War Production in Pictures*, 1946.

Bird, Vivian: *Portrait of Birmingham*, Hale: 1970.

Bowyer, Michael J F; *Action Stations Vol.6 - Military Airfields of the Cotswolds and the Central Midlands*, Patrick Stephens: Cambridge 1983.

Brazier, R H, and Sadford, E: *Birmingham and the Great War 1914-19*, Cornish Brothers: Birmingham, 1921.

Bruce, J M: *S.E.5A - Fighter Supreme*, serialised in the *Aeroplane Monthly*, May - November 1977.

Bruce, J M: *Austin's Agressor* (Austin A.F.B.1) from *Aeroplane Monthly* 1978 pp603-7, 668-73.

Bruce, J M: *The Aeroplanes of the Royal Flying Corps (Military Wing)*, Putnam: London 1982.

Cavallo, Tiberius: *The History and Practice of Aerostation*, 1785.

Church, Roy: *Herbert Austin - The British Motor Car Industry to 1941*, (In particular on shadow factory negotiations) Europa: 1979.

Collier, B: *The Airship*, Hart-Davis, MacGibbon 1974.

Cramp, B G: *British Midland Airways*, Airline Publications and Sales: Hounslow 1979.

Cross, R: *Lord Swinton*, Oxford University Press: 1982

Dunphy, Angus: *The West Midlands Airfields*, Ellows Hall School and Dudley Teachers Centre: 1978.

Fairfax, Ernest: *Calling All Arms*, Hutchinson.

Faulkner, J N: *British Railways and Civil Aviation 1929-48*, (article in *Railway World*, February 1978).

Gilbert, M: *Finest Hour: Winston S Churchill 1939-41*, William Heinemann: London, 1983.

Gomersall, Bryce: *The Stirling File*, Air-Britain/Aviation Archaeologists Publications 1979.

Henshaw, Alex: *Sigh for a Merlin*, John Murray 1979.

Hunt, Leslie: *Twenty-One Squadrons*, (re 605 Sqn), Garnstone Press: 1972.

Lambert, Z E and Wyatt, R E: *Lord Austin - The Man*, Sidgwick & Jackson: 1968.

Mackay, James: *Airmails 1870-1970*, Batsford: 1971.

Mason, Francis K: *Battle over Britain*, McWhirter: 1969

Moss, Peter W: *British Civil Aircraft Registers 1919-28* and *British Civil Aircraft Registers 1928-30*, Air-Britain: 1969 and 1971 respectiveley.

Newell, M D: *Castle Bromwich - its Airfield and Aircraft Factory*, Enthusiasts Publications: 1982.

Nixon, St John C: *Wolseley: A Saga of the Motor Industry*, Marshall Press: 1949.

Nockolds, Harold: *Lucas: The First 100 Years*, 2 vols, David & Charles: 1976 and 1978.

Overy, R J: *William Morris - Viscount Nuffield*, Europa

Price, Alfred: *Spitfire at War* (In particular the chapter *Production Testing* by Alex Henshaw MBE). Ian Allan: Shepperton 1974.

Read, Colin E: *Dunlop's Test Flight*, Air-Britain *Aeromilitaria* magazine 1983 p43.

Riding, E J: *The Austin Whippet* (article in the *Aeromodeller* May 1945).

Robertson, Bruce: *Spitfire - Story of a Famous Fighter* Harleyford: 1960.

Robertson, Bruce: *Lancaster - Story of a Famous Bomber*, Harleyford: 1964.

Robson, Graham: *The Rover Story*, Patrick Stephens: Cambridge (2nd edition) 1981.

Rolt, L T C: *The Aeronauts (A History of Ballooning 1783-1903)*.

Scott, J D: *Vickers: A History*, Weidenfeld & Nicolson.

Stroud, John: *Annals of British and Commonwealth Air Transport*, Putnam: London 1961.

Sutcliffe, Anthony, and Smith, Roger: *Birmingham 1939-70*, Oxford: 1974.

Taylor, A J P: *Beaverbrook*, Hamish Hamilton: 1972.

Tibbles, A J: *The Rise of Birmingham Music Festivals 1768-1854*, (BA dissertation, University of Birmingham 1970).

Wakefield, Kenneth: *The First Pathfinders*, (history of Kampfgruppe 100, 1939-41), William Kimber: London 1981.

Wyatt, R J: *The Austin 1905-52*, David & Charles 1981.

The following journals and newspapers were also consulted: *Aeromilitaria* (Air-Britain), *Aeroplane Monthly*, *Aircraft Illustrated*, *Air Pictorial*, *Archive* (Air-Britain), *Birmingham Evening Mail*, *Birmingham Post*, *Coventry Evening Telegraph*, *Flight (later Flight International)*, *Vintage Aircraft*.